HOPE & HEARTBREAK:

BEYOND THE NUMBERS OF THE OPIOID EPIDEMIC.

HOPE & HEARTBREAK:

BEYOND THE NUMBERS OF THE OPIOID EPIDEMIC.

SCOTT BROWN

ISBN 978-1-7336616-0-7 (paperback)

ISBN 978-1-7336616-1-4 (ebook)

Published by Red Mark Publishing.

Printed in the United States of America.

TABLE OF CONTENTS

In memory of Brandon Bernett, Sage Capozzi, and Casey Schwartzmier. I never met Brandon, Sage, or Casey, all of whom battled addiction before succumbing to the disease. After hearing a lot about each of them, I know that they were good kids who made a mistake. And they are missed every day by their loved ones.

ACKNOWLEDGMENTS

I set out to write a book about the opioid epidemic from the people who live it. I wanted their experiences and stories to address issues, such as stigma and treatment of addiction to the stress it puts on families and first responders and the struggle for those in addiction and those left behind by overdose deaths. I wanted them to humanize this awful scourge, and they did that. I was simply fortunate enough to tell their stories and put together a book that gives a comprehensive look at the opioid epidemic. I couldn't have done it without the cooperation of so many people, including some who were gracious enough to relive stories that are still painful to tell. I interviewed closed to ninety people for the book and conducted well over one hundred interviews. To those who helped with interviews, I am truly grateful. You didn't just allow me to tell an important story. You educated me, too.

Those who gave multiple interviews and were patient with my constant questions: Carmen Capozzi, Dawn and Rick Hennessey, Tony Marcocci, Shannon Moore, Tim Phillips, Greg Powell, Katrin Schall, Michelle Schwartzmier, Diana Shea, and VonZell Wade and Laurie Johnson-Wade.

Others who gave interviews: Christine Ackerman, Mike Baacke, Ken Bacha, Kristi Batzel, Elizabeth Beck, Meagan Bilik-DeFazio, Beth

Bitler, Howie Boelky, James Bumar, Dona Cardiff, Gina Cerilli, Elizabeth Comer, Robert Derry, Gus DiRenna, Justin Drish, Christopher Feliciani, Bona Ferluckaj, John Gallagher, Adam Garrity, Rege Garris, Jay Geisler, Bonnie Guldenschuh, Patty Graf, Jonathan Han, Carolyn Harr, Austin Hixson, Jeff Held, Randy Highlands, Becky Hubert, Colleen Hughes, David Humes, Avi Israel, Lorie Johnson, Chris Jones, Rich Jones, Clark Kerr, Kim Klingensmith, Eric Kocian, Richard Kosisko, Dorine and Rena Kozemchak, Georgette and Joe Lehr, Dave Lewis, Kelley Lord, David Lettrich, Carol Lubovinsky, Edward Malesic, Joyce Maybach, Paul Niemiec, Barb Penn, Elba Ramos, Nikki Reed, Josh Rimmel, Ashley Rudnik, Shara Saveikis, Jason Slonceski, Eileen Smith, Tony "Pap" Sobotka, Tim Sobota, Connie Staley, Mike Stangroom, Joyce Sterling, Sharon Stinebiser, Terry Struble, Bree Swarmer, Teresa Takach, Henry Taliercio, Gary Tennis, Mark Vega, Della Utberg, William Urbanik, Stephanie Walker, and Pat Williams.

A special thanks to Kevin Stevens for writing the introduction as well as Kelli Wilson and Andy Bernstein for helping to make it happen.

Finally, thanks to my family and friends who were so supportive. My sister, Ali Finer, kicked my butt editing the first draft of this but made it so much better. Even cooler is that she learned a lot of stuff she didn't know. My dad, Scott, constantly supplied me with news articles, some of which led to interviews, and he had some great ideas as well.

FOREWORD

I was twenty-eight years old and on top of the world. I had just won two Stanley Cups with the Pittsburgh Penguins. I was a first-team, All-NHL pick in the 1991–92 season, when we successfully defended our Stanley Cup title. The next season we were playing in New York City and I went out with some of the guys for a couple of beers. We walked into a club and someone handed me something. I know now it was cocaine, but at the time I had never done a drug in my life. I thought trying this drug would just be a one-shot thing. I was young. I was bulletproof. It took me about twenty seconds to make a decision that changed the course of my life.

Twenty-two years later, I wake up every morning and remind myself that I am a drug addict. It's a hard truth, but my brain is wired just like the addict who is homeless and sitting on the street corner. The only difference between the addict who has lost everything and me is that I'm sober and living the life I'm supposed to live. I am no better than any other addict.

I have been clean for two years and four months, and it is a far easier way to live my life. Being addicted to drugs is a full-time job. It's so hard, and until you find a way to stop, it will take everything that you have. I lost my family and got a divorce because of my addiction. I lost a lot of my money. I could have easily lost my life.

Cocaine activated something in my brain, but my descent into addiction was gradual. Three months after I tried cocaine, I suffered a serious injury when I got my face planted in the ice during a playoff game. I needed reconstruction surgery, and that was my introduction to pain medication. I didn't get hooked on pain medication then, however. Using cocaine sporadically, but at the absolute wrong time, is what hastened my exit from Pittsburgh. I started getting traded because to play at a first-team All-NHL level, you must focus 100 percent on hockey. I didn't do that. I played for four different teams after Pittsburgh traded me in 1995. I returned to the Penguins for my final two NHL seasons before retiring in 2002.

I loved Pittsburgh and loved playing for the Penguins and on Mario Lemieux's line. I should have played my entire career there and won more Stanley Cups. But that's what this disease does. It starts to take and take and take. For me, it took things slowly but methodically.

Not long after I retired, I hurt my neck at the gym. The next thing I knew I was doing pain pills. They were easy for me to get since I could say I needed them for pain or injuries that lingered from a seventeen-year NHL career. And I didn't discriminate. I took Percocet and Oxycontin (brand names for oxycodone) and even heroin. Everyone thinks heroin is so bad, but pain medication is the same thing. People run out of money, and they go to heroin because it is cheaper to buy. Once I got sucked into opiate use, I couldn't stop. I had stints of sobriety but nothing long-term.

I tried to stop on my own, but addiction is way more powerful than anyone. The average person doesn't understand addiction. It's not about willpower. It's not about just stopping. The disease doesn't allow you to do that until you find the solution. As much as you want to be a good dad, as much as you want to be a good husband, it just doesn't allow you to be that person. And when you're trapped in the disease, you don't see it. You don't see what you're doing to other people in your life. All you think is, "How am I not going to be sick the next day?" That is what keeps you using after you become stuck in addiction.

The end of my former life started the day the FBI kicked my door in and arrested me for drug possession and intent to deliver. Everything that led to that day could be traced to one thing: I needed pain medication to feed my habit. I sat in jail for a week and resolved to change my life. A lot of help and support after I chose life over addiction basically saved me.

I now live a day at a time and go to Alcoholics Anonymous meetings every day. I used to chase drugs for seven hours a day. There is no reason why I can't spend an hour a day at a meeting, especially since the meetings make me feel better. I have made a lot of friends through the fellowship and shared experiences of Alcoholics Anonymous. It's important for me to be around those people because it reminds me who I am. It's a very simple way to live, and I work on my sobriety every day. I still have friends who drink, and I'm at the point now where it doesn't bother me. But I don't hang around bars. And if I golf, I go home afterward instead of stopping in the clubhouse.

You've got to find a different way to live that makes you happy, and I have. I love my life, and I'm lucky. In my two-plus years in recovery, I got back most of the things I lost that were important to me, like family and friends. I am back with the Penguins, working as a scout in the New England area. My greater purpose may be the work I do with Power Forward, the nonprofit foundation I started in January 2018, with Andy Bernstein and Kelli Wilson, my sister. We help people get into treatment, raise awareness, teach prevention, and attack stigma. Ending the stigma attached to addiction is so important because, even in the midst of this epidemic, so many people don't want to talk about or acknowledge it. One of the ways my foundation addresses this is through my weekly radio show, Cross Check, which fosters honest discussion about addiction and highlights success stories and ways for people to get help.

Parents don't think it's ever going to be their kid who gets sucked into addiction. I don't think it's going to be *my* kids. They know what I've gone through, but I never pulled them aside and said, "Let's talk about drugs." My three kids are phenomenal. They're good people; they're athletes, and yet I pray to God that they never get into drugs.

I tell my story publicly all the time, and while I can't get anybody sober, I can tell them how I made one decision that changed the path of my life. Nobody thinks it's going to be them who gets hooked or dies. It's a sneaky, sneaky disease, and it can grab anybody. I'm a perfect example of that. If you wanted someone's life before I tried cocaine, it was mine. I was a successful hockey player at the highest level of a tough sport. And yet that was ultimately no match for my addiction. If I hadn't surrendered to it and kept doing what I was doing I would be dead right now.

—Kevin Stevens

Kevin Stevens played in the NHL from 1987–2002 and was one of the driving forces behind the Pittsburgh Penguins winning the first two Stanley Cups in club history. He played in three NHL All-Star games during his career, and his best season came in 1991–92. He scored 123 points, the most ever by an American-born NHL player, cementing his status as one of the premier wingers in the game. Among Stevens's career superlatives, his seventeen goals in the 1990–91 playoffs are tied for the fourth-most in NHL history. He lives in Kingston, Massachusetts, and scouts college players and free agents for the Penguins. For more information on Power Forward, go to www.Powerforward25.com.

PROLOGUE

The price of the opioid epidemic transcended dollars on this wintry, mid-March day in 2018. Inside of Brooks Funeral Home in Mt. Pleasant, a small borough in the rolling hills and farmland of Western Pennsylvania, that toll could be measured by things much more visceral than numbers.

A young man leaned over a casket and kissed the forehead of Amanda Hixson before he and the other pallbearers received final instructions. Tissue boxes were passed back and forth among those who had gathered to say goodbye to the twenty-six-year-old mother of three. The sniffling and occasional gasping for breath did not stop after "Amazing Grace" played, underscoring Rev. Richard Kosisko's impossible task of making sense of the senseless within the parameters of a funeral service.

Kosisko tried to provide comfort by referencing the collage of pictures that flanked the casket at the front of the room.

"I'm sure stories that go with these pictures on this very difficult day brought great joy and will continue to bring joy," he said. "But we also know it brings a deep hurt to our hearts. We celebrate Amanda's life as we come together today. The days of joy and great strength, but also the days we know were difficult for her. She is at peace. She is at rest. No more pain or confusion or distractions or darkness in her life."

The confusion and pain will endure for those she left behind. Nothing illustrated this more than what took place right after the service. A young boy wearing a red hooded sweatshirt and black pants stood in a waiting area close enough to the funeral home's entrance that you could hear the strain of bagpipes. He wiped tears from his eyes as an older woman wrapped him in a hug.

"We are so lucky," she said to him, "because we both have mommas who are angels."

That haunting scene stuck with me as I drove north on Route 819, a road I traveled a handful of times in 2017-18 as I chronicled the opioid epidemic. I received some context to it when I later met with Amanda's mother, Carol Lubovinsky.

Through tears, she told me that the funeral wasn't the first time that Bobby, the nine-year-old boy I saw after the funeral, cried over the loss of his mother. She talked about Amanda's battle with the "devil" and how she had been clean for more than a year before she overdosed—shortly after regaining custody of her two-year-old daughter. Amanda, in fact, had been preparing a meal for her daughter, Lizzy, when heroin laced with fentanyl killed her.

Carol dabbed at her eyes much more than she touched her Reuben sandwich during our ninety-minute lunch. Her hands fidgeted, and she broke down several times during the interview. The first time happened after she talked about how well Amanda had been doing and how the long-range goal was to reunite her with Bobby, and her younger son, Eban.

Carol won full custody of the boys five years earlier after realizing the extent of Amanda's drug problem. She went to the Westmoreland County Courthouse the day after watching Amanda fall asleep three times while changing Eban's diaper. Carol has been her grandsons' full-time caretaker ever since then. You could see the stress of dealing with a child in addiction in Carol's blue eyes. They were as weary as they were sad. Nothing better captured the strain she experienced then when she told me about one of Amanda's visits with her sons.

It happened on Easter weekend 2014 when Amanda stole $15,000 worth of jewelry from Carol's house. Much of it belonged to the late wife of her husband. Amanda also took a ring she had once given to Carol for Mother's Day. It was gold plated and contained the birthstones of Bobby and Eban.

The stories Carol told me that day showed why the opioid epidemic goes beyond numbers. There are those left behind, be it grieving parents or confused children who may feel abandoned. There is addiction itself and what it causes people to do to feed it. Stealing and other addiction-related crimes tear apart families and fill prisons to their breaking point.

"It's the biggest issue facing us," Westmoreland County Commissioner Gina Cerilli told me of the opioid epidemic, "and nobody has an answer how to fix it."

* * *

There were approximately 64,000 drug overdose deaths in 2016 in the United States, according to the National Institute on Drug Abuse. Or, as Cerilli framed it, "That's like three commercial jets falling out of the sky every single week." That year also produced more opioid-related fatalities in the United States than the deadliest year of the Vietnam War, according to *The Washington Post*. That war touched off mass demonstrations and protests because of the carnage and spawned a national movement.

That year, I really started notice what was going on around me. It seemed like every time I turned on the news or looked at a newspaper, there was something about an overdose death or the opioid epidemic. One day, in 2017, I flipped through the latest edition of *Sports Illustrated*. On the back page was a column written by Rex Chapman. The former NBA player became addicted to opiates during a playing career that included ten surgeries. He became an activist in recovery, and he issued a national call to action, particularly in his home state of Kentucky.

Six months later, I started working full-time on chronicling the opioid epidemic in Western Pennsylvania, with an emphasis on Westmoreland County. I originally planned to just focus on the county where I grew up and live today. But the epidemic doesn't recognize borders any more than it does age, race, gender, and socioeconomic status. And my reporting inevitably led me outside of Westmoreland County and Pennsylvania.

Two things I quickly learned is that I was way late in waking up to the opioid epidemic—and that it had hit particularly hard right outside of my front door. Drug and alcohol deaths in Westmoreland County increased 537 percent from 2002 to 2017, according to the county coroner's office. That unfathomable spike was fueled by prescription drugs, heroin, and, more recently fentanyl and carfentanil.

Westmoreland County started tracking overdose deaths in 2002, the year coroner Ken Bacha took office. To put into perspective what he has dealt with, including 193 overdose deaths in 2017, consider this: "My dad (Leo) was coroner for twenty-four years before me, and he had five heroin overdoses," Bacha said. "I had twelve my first year."

The box that Shannon Moore keeps in her Latrobe apartment is one morbid marker of the devastation wrought by the opioid epidemic. It's filled with over 200 obituaries of people she knew. Many of the deaths were drug related.

"I need another box," said Shannon, a recovering addict. "It sucks."

Overdose deaths were significantly down in Westmoreland and surrounding counties through the first half of 2018. But it was too early to tell whether that represented significant progress or whether the widespread availability of Narcan, a drug that reverses the effects of overdoses, has led to the decrease in overdose deaths.

Narcan is now so prevalent that a handful of Westmoreland County libraries carry it in case of an overdose. Libraries stocked with Narcan should be shocking. But the Centers for Disease Control and Prevention (CDC) found that heroin use among eighteen- to twenty-five-year-olds increased by 109 percent from 2002 to 2013 and increased by 100 percent among females during that span. Small wonder then that Narcan has found its way into the unlikeliest of places.

There are so many numbers and statistics that tell the story of the opioid epidemic but only part of it. I wanted to capture the stories behind those numbers, to give them context, to humanize them. That drew me to Michelle Schwartzmier, who lost her twenty-year-old daughter, Casey, to an overdose on January 15, 2017.

"There are a lot of numbers," said Michelle, who lives in the North Hills of Pittsburgh. "I could tell you about my son, Casey's seventeen-year-old brother, who carried her casket. How about that number, seventeen? Does that get your attention? Casey was a person. She wasn't a junkie, a loser, a troll under a bridge. She was my daughter. A part of me died with her."

Michelle said this inside of a hushed Rogers Center at St. Vincent College in Latrobe, almost a year after losing her only daughter. She spoke as part of *GOAL Magazine's* symposium on the opioid epidemic, an event that attracted hundreds of people.

Michelle talked about a letter Casey wrote her for their final Christmas together because she couldn't afford to buy a present. The letter told Michelle how proud Casey was going to make her and about the career and kids she planned to have after she got her life back on track. She shared that Casey overdosed next to a suitcase that was packed for her trip to a drug and alcohol treatment center in California the following day.

She talked about how hope was Casey's favorite word and how that led to the promise that Michelle fulfilled after Casey died. Casey had asked her mother to write an honest obituary if anything happened to her, to give hope to the countless others out there and to let them know they are not alone in their struggle. The obituary went viral and even reached the White House.

"What started out as a mother—daughter promise has turned into a legacy," Michelle said. "I'm not going to sit in shame and hide. Casey's story ended in tragedy, and if it makes you sad, I'm sorry. If it makes you angry, good because emotions can be a powerful tool, and we need every tool we can get in this war."

That night as I drove home, I stopped at a red light on Route 30, a couple of miles from St. Vincent College. On the other side of the highway, a car sat surrounded by other vehicles with flashing blue lights. What looked like a minor accident had drawn a handful of responders. Normally, I wouldn't have given it a second thought. But

I had just spent a couple of hours listening to people on the front lines of the opioid epidemic. I looked at those flashing lights and wondered if they served as some sort of metaphor.

Are we in the middle of an emergency yet lack a blue lights response to it?

*   *   *

The cost of the opioid epidemic came to light in a sleepy auditorium, four days before Christmas, 2017. Carmen Capozzi, clad in a black Sage's Army T-shirt, flannel shirt, and blue jeans, stood in front of West Mifflin Senior High School students and asked for their help. Behind him a collage of pictures flashed onto a screen. There was Sage in his senior picture. There was Sage playing in his band. There were Sage and Carmen with their arms around one another.

Carmen told the students how Sage died at the age of twenty from a heroin overdose, how he was a talented musician who also loved to golf, how the girlfriend sitting on the swing with him in one of the pictures had recently been arrested following a string of armed robberies—and how she was currently sitting in the Allegheny County Prison facing serious prison time (I later learned from Carmen that she was more afraid to be out of jail than be in it because of her addiction).

"You're the generation of change," Carmen told the students. "You can help make a difference."

Carmen returned to the girl on the swing and talked about the time he walked past Sage's bedroom, saw her shooting a video, and asked what they were doing. Sage told him he was telling his story for her senior project at Norwin High School about addiction. "Absolutely not," Carmen told him. "Worry about yourself." Sage retorted that if it helped one person, it was worth it. Carmen again told him to worry about himself. Case closed.

A month after Sage died on March 5, 2012, Carmen wanted to spread awareness at Norwin. One of Sage's English teachers told him to show the video of Sage talking about addiction. Video? What video? Carmen had no idea that Sage had defied his order.

More than five years later, Carmen played that video for the West Mifflin students, just as he has done during scores of speeches and presentations since Sage's death.

He watched with everyone else in the auditorium as Sage talked about how drug use had led to expulsion from Norwin, to the arrest that landed him in a facility for juvenile offenders, and to the embarrassment he felt of being labeled an addict. Sage credited getting sent away as a juvenile for saving him from himself.

"It's hard being away from people, like not having all of the freedoms but it's worth it in the end," Sage said in the video. "I'd probably be in worse positions than I was. I probably wouldn't be in school. I wouldn't have my GED and might be in jail . . ."

This is where Carmen interrupted.

"He never thought he would die. He thought the worst thing that would happen to him was jail. Nobody thinks they're going to die."

That was still on Carmen's mind after Sage's video ended.

"I miss my kid every day," he said. "I walk by his room every day and wonder who he would be today. Would he be married? Would he have kids? Would he have a job, or would he still be on drugs? I don't know. Heroin killed my son, but you know what started it? Bad coping skills. I lost my mom to cancer, and Sage was very close with his grandmother. You know what he decided? Screw it. I'm going to go get high. He shot heroin and died."

What didn't die with Sage was his hope that his story could help others. Carmen started Sage's Army with his longtime partner, Cindy Noll, and her mother, who was like a grandmother to Sage. He built the grassroots organization with sheer will and an I'll-be-damned-if-I-stay-quiet mindset that coalesced after suffering the worst loss imaginable for a parent.

I spent more time with Carmen than anyone else during my reporting, including two trips to Harrisburg. One was for a state Drug and Alcohol Advisory Board meeting and another for work with state Rep. Eric Nelson on an addiction treatment bill. During those drives, Carmen talked to a handful of addicts over the phone and made subsequent follow-up calls to get them into treatment. It can be pretty daunting for someone who wants help but doesn't know what the hell to do beyond asking for it. Carmen guided them with a patient and reassuring touch, and those types of calls are a part of his days now.

Sage's Army helps put addicts on the road to recovery through a twenty-four-hour helpline. It holds grief and family support sessions in its downtown Irwin headquarters. Carmen speaks at schools, prisons, and treatment facilities—anywhere really. He choked back tears at a Greensburg restaurant one day while telling his story to local religious leaders who had convened to talk about turning prayer into action.

Imagine reliving the worst experience of your life, doing it over and over and doing it when you could have said it's not your problem any-more after the loss of your only child. That was Carmen's life, and it caught up with him shortly before the sixth anniversary of Sage's death.

The lines between activist and grieving father didn't just blur. They collided while Carmen was in Harrisburg for a parent/coach training session. The group was about thirty seconds out of a meditation ex-ercise when a sharp pain jabbed Carmen. His stomach did a flip and a wave of grief crashed into him. Carmen jumped up from the table in the hotel conference room. He had just made it to the entrance when he completely broke down. He pushed through the door, and the screaming and wailing continued in the hallway.

The two women running the sessions helped him to a nearby seat. He cried so hard that he had trouble catching his breath. One of the women was a mental health counselor, and she asked him to explain what was happening as he rocked back and forth. He told her it was happening all over again.

The call he received from the police after Sage overdosed in a motel room. Walking into the hospital and fearing the worst. The pain he experienced when he lost Sage.

Six years later it still hurt like hell.

AN ENORMOUS COST

NOBODY DESERVES THIS

It would be hard to find someone who has suffered more from the opioid epidemic than Sharon Stinebiser. She lost both of her sons, her only two children, to overdoses within a span of seven hours. Both overdoses happened in the Youngwood home where she still lives with her dog, Crosby. It is less than a mile from where Joshaua Gunther and Dylan Fisher are buried, side by side, in the Youngwood Cemetery.

"They were my everything," Sharon said.

We met almost two years after Sharon lost her sons and less than a week after she celebrated her forty-fifth birthday. Her hands shook at times as she told her story. But she also smiled when she recalled how close her sons were, despite being such opposites, and how Sundays were always their day. They would gather in her kitchen and make piles of scrambled eggs to go with home fries, bacon, ham, and sausage. Sometimes they switched it up and made French toast, Belgian waffles, or pancakes to go with the sides. They sat down together and just talked over a feast, enjoying each other's company.

"I think of the good times," Sharon said.

I wondered, with those memories and many others, why she stays in the house where she lost her sons. But then she never gets away from what happened, no matter where she is. That became clear as she talked about her work with people suffering from dementia.

"They will ask me on a daily basis how my kids are doing," Sharon said. "You tell them once (what happened), and you tell them again, and then you get to a point where you just say they're fine. They don't mean to be like that, and I know that. I get depressed when I go to work sometimes, especially when I see some of these older people who have no family. I sit there and think that's going to be me."

What is particularly heartbreaking about Sharon's story is she thought her family had made it through the hell of addiction. Josh battled it for years, and his love for his younger brother finally inspired him to get clean.

Josh went to a treatment facility and moved in with his grandparents to get a fresh start. He got a job a DeLallo's, a Jeannette supermarket specializing in Italian food, as a warehouse operator and worked his way up. He eventually moved into a supervisor position. He had been clean for more than eight years when his brother found him unresponsive on the night of April 6, 2016. Dylan woke Sharon in a panic. She called 911 and performed CPR on Josh. The paramedics arrived shortly after her 10 p.m. phone call, but there wasn't much they could do. Josh was pronounced dead at 11:59 p.m. Sharon did her best to hold it together because Dylan was seething with anger. She tried to talk to him but finally went to bed around 2:30 a.m.

"The last words he said to me were, 'I love you, Mom, but please get the f away from me right now,'" she said. "I said, 'OK, that's fine. You need time alone. I understand.'"

Sharon got up at 5 a.m. to check on Dylan only to find that he had overdosed. Paramedics returned to the house, but Dylan was pronounced dead at 7 a.m. on April 7.

"I don't know if he knew what he was taking, and it was an accident, or if it was suicide," Sharon said. "I'll never know because he never had a drug issue in his life."

Sharon stood between the caskets at the viewings for Josh and Dylan. She had Dylan laid out in a suit; Josh was dressed in a St. Patrick's Day hooded sweatshirt, baseball hat, and jeans. That's just who her sons were: total opposites. That they were so different is still a source of laughter—and comfort—for Sharon.

Josh loved sports while Dylan was drawn to the arts. He started working on a science-fiction book after Sharon encouraged him to chase his dreams, and he embraced the spotlight.

"He was the class clown," Sharon said. "Everybody loved him because he was the outgoing, friendly, lovable person who was friends with everybody. He loved to be the center of attention. Josh was the opposite. They evened each other out. They were awesome together. I think that's why they were so close."

That closeness can be seen in the locket that hangs from Sharon's neck. Inside of it is a picture of Josh and Dylan with their arms around one another. That is not all that Sharon does to stay close to her sons. She wears their socks, jackets, and T-shirts. In a picture that ran on the front page of the *Tribune-Review* on December 29, 2017, Sharon wore a gray pullover. The DeLallo's logo and the fact that it is a little big on her gives away that it was Josh's sweatshirt. She wore it for a story titled "A Decade of Death," which detailed the destruction that the opioid epidemic has wrought in Westmoreland County.

Sharon Stinebiser flanked by sons Josh Gunther and Dylan Fisher. Photo courtesy of Sharon Stinebiser.

Sharon tells her tragic story with the hopes that others won't have to live it. She has spoken at schools, prisons, and a Students Against Drunk Driving (SADD) convention. She has also worked with Robert

Reed, the executive attorney general under Pennsylvania attorney general Josh Shapiro, to bring awareness to the opioid epidemic.

"I don't want to see anybody go through this," she said. "Even that short moment when I saw how Dylan reacted to losing his brother was heartbreaking. Nobody deserves this. Nobody. As long as people will listen to me, I'll do whatever I can."

The unfortunate reality is that Sharon knows she is not alone. Thirty people from Josh's graduating class at Norwin High School have fatally overdosed, she said. When a friend of hers ran across a news story about a mother who lost two sons to overdoses, she assumed it was about Sharon.

Instead, it was about a Wisconsin woman who lost her sons on April 9, 2016. Sharon contacted her, and the two stay in touch and check on each other. When she reads the obituaries—she does it daily despite her losses—and sees ones for people in their twenties and thirties, it reinforces why she is so open about her story. She wants her sons to be proud of her and knows that they would want her to help.

"They would do anything for their friends or people in general," she said. "They would be so mad at me if I just stayed at home, miserable."

One of Sharon's favorite things to wear is a green hooded sweatshirt that says, "Show me your shamrocks." It was typical Josh humor. St. Patrick's Day was Josh's favorite holiday and he and his friends always celebrated it in Pittsburgh. He had planned to take Dylan with them in 2017 since it would have been his first St. Patrick's Day at the age of twenty-one, the legal drinking age.

They never got the opportunity, which makes St. Patrick's Day part of an emotional gauntlet for Sharon as it falls in a six-month period that is filled with holidays, birthdays, and the death of her sons.

"November, December, January, February, March, and April are my bad months," she said. "As soon as April is over, I start breathing."

RIPPLE EFFECTS

A few taps on her cell phone was all it took for Kim Klingensmith to provide snapshots of addiction.

A video showed her son, unaware that she was taping him, standing with his eyes closed and his head bowed. His three-year-old daughter said, "Oh look. Daddy sleepy again." He walked zombie-like toward a couch with a syringe tucked behind his left ear, as if it was something as benign as a pencil, while Kim told him she was not "putting up with it anymore."

He looked up after a few seconds, and his face twisted into a mask of anger.

The scene ended with Kim's son snarling at her and lunging unsteadily at the phone. Kim had taken the video a couple of weeks earlier, and it wasn't the first time she had done something like that. "I have many videos of both of my kids," the Vandergrift resident said.

Becky Hubert could relate. All four of her children were in prison at the time, three of them for crimes tied to heroin addiction.

"Obviously I don't sleep," Becky said, referencing the dark lines under her eyes. "My mind keeps going, *OK, what else can I do? What's the next step?* You don't know who they are because it's not them."

Here is the thing: Kim and Becky were the lucky ones the day I met with them and Della Utberg at Creekside Diner in Apollo. At least they still had their kids.

Della lost her son, Bryan Hall, to a fentanyl overdose in 2016, four days before Christmas. Bryan served in the Marine Corps. He also spent two years in nursing school before his drug use escalated and ultimately killed him at the age of twenty-eight. He left behind two young children and a grieving mother who battled through the courts, so she could have custody of her two grandchildren every other weekend.

"It has permanently ripped my family apart," Della said of losing Bryan. "There's damage that won't heal because he's not there. It's too late."

Creekside Diner is just off Route 66, a pie's throw from the highway that winds through most of Westmoreland County. The inside of the diner is quaint with a signature counter and a menu that is most diner-esque of all: everything is reasonably priced and probably good. Kim, Becky, Della, and I talked for more than two hours in a relaxed setting. It was a distinct contrast to the angst-ridden stories that illustrated the collateral damage of the opioid epidemic.

Two of the three women had some form of custody of at least one grandchild and had filed emergency custody petitions because they feared for their grandchild's safety. Two of the three had at least one child in prison. All three had ridden the rollercoaster of addiction through their children.

"This isn't just a child's disease," Becky said.

Kim knows that better than most. Both of her sons have battled a heroin addiction for years, and the strain she lives with is as consistent as the sun rising. She is used to finding empty stamp bags and syringes around the house. Her husband, the stepfather to her sons, has given her a me-or-them ultimatum more than once.

One of her sons has been to rehab twelve times. The other son has been in jail and, in his mid-twenties, already bears the physical hallmarks of addiction: sunken cheeks and rotting teeth. Once, one of her sons had to give the other Narcan after he overdosed while riding in the back of a car with children in it. The nadir for Kim came when she watched one of her sons shoot up after taking him to buy heroin.

"I bawled my eyes out," she said.

She did the unthinkable out of a mother's desperation to keep her child alive.

Her son had been accepted to a treatment facility but had to wait a couple of days until a bed became available. He told Kim he needed heroin to keep from getting dope sick. She reluctantly consented to it on two conditions: he bought only enough heroin to maintain, and she supervised when he used.

Kim knows it sounds crazy, but she worried that he might run if she didn't relent. Nothing better sums up what it is like loving an addict than having to make what Kim saw as the better of two awful choices.

"It has made me someone I'm not," she said of living with addiction. "I'm embarrassed for me."

She deals with more than embarrassment. Kim is raising a granddaughter, at the age of forty-nine, while also dealing with Multiple sclerosis. Her granddaughter is one of more than 2.5 million kids in the United States who are being raised by a relative instead of a parent because of substance abuse, according to Generations United.

"It's a lot harder chasing after a three-year-old than it was when my kids were three," Kim said. "It (MS) adds physical issues. There are times I'd like to give her back, but this is what we had to do to keep her safe."

Kim is fortunate that a lot has fallen into place since gaining full custody of her granddaughter. Her boss allowed her to switch her schedule, so she could work opposite of her husband. One of them is able to stay home except for the few hours when their shifts overlap. They have a neighbor who babysits during those times for a minimal fee, which is also crucial since they can't afford daycare.

"It's difficult," Kim said. "Sometimes, it's the simplest thing like, *Wow, my body can't take this anymore.* I can't sleep when I need to, and it can be tough trying to figure out schedules."

What worries Kim most is how growing up with a father in addiction—and in a home filled with tension—has affected her granddaughter, who sometimes announces that she is going to pray for her daddy.

"In her sweet, childish voice," Kim said, "she'll say, 'Dear God please bless Daddy. Amen.'"

Her father was in jail for theft the day I met with Kim, Becky, and Della. One week later, Kim was already finding it hard to evade questions from her granddaughter.

"She asks every day, 'When is daddy coming home? Where's daddy at?' I don't know what to tell her," Kim said. "When she asks it now, I just say, 'I don't know honey. I know you miss him and I'm sure he really misses you right now.' I want to get her into counseling, so I know how to answer these questions."

Kim's willingness to tell her story—"I'll shout it from the mountaintop if I can bring awareness"—is matched by Becky.

"I have no problem telling people I am a mother of addicts," she said. "I'm sad for that aspect, not for me but (for) my children. I used to deny their addiction, but I will never do it again."

Becky had recently become a chairperson for Residents Against Illicit Drugs, an Armstrong County-based organization that promotes education and awareness and provides support to those impacted by addiction. She also runs a Facebook page called Heroin Education Awareness and Revival.

She is a no-nonsense, outspoken woman. What also makes her perfect for the grassroots activism that is critical to battling the opioid epidemic: she is a pissed-off parent.

"I've been to four funerals of my kids' friends. My heart breaks for their parents," Becky said. "I got to a point where I was going to be damned if I was going to lose my child, especially to the demon."

Unfortunately, she is way too intimate with that demon. She saw one son relapse after he had been clean for twenty-three months. Another son relapsed after he had been clean for more than two years.

Becky has gone through denial, guilt, and desperation. One time she set up her own daughter for a possible arrest after she couldn't get in contact with her and feared she was on a binge. Becky offered a $50 reward on Facebook if someone called the Vandergrift Police Department about her daughter, who had a handful of outstanding warrants. She guessed, correctly, that some of her daughter's so-called friends would jump at the chance for money to pay for a fix. Becky's phone was "blowing up" within fifteen minutes of posting the reward offer. She called the police and told them where they could find her daughter.

Becky said one of the hardest things about dealing with addiction is watching your children turn into people you don't know. That is why she found hope in a jailhouse conversation she had with her daughter the previous day. She had called to wish her a happy birthday and to lift her spirits since she was spending it in prison. She got a gift of her own from the phone call when she had a lucid conversation with her daughter.

"I didn't hear the ramblings. I didn't hear excuse after excuse," Becky said. "I heard my daughter, and that was the best thing on her thirty-second birthday. I thank God every day that she is alive and that I can go to a jail and visit my child."

COMPASSION AND ACTION

The call came after midnight, and Dawn Hennessey sprang into action. She grabbed her car keys and rode off into the night. The call was from grandparents who had custody of twin grandsons suffering from neonatal abstinence syndrome (NAS). Dawn had given them her cell phone number and told them to use it any time they felt overwhelmed. The distress call came as she was sleeping, so Dawn could be excused for running out of the house without her purse. She didn't anticipate having to explain why she was driving in a bathrobe and without her license at 1 a.m. after she got pulled over for a broken taillight.

She explained the story to the police officer and added, "I can show you the baby on the way back."

He let her go, and if anyone deserves a little understanding it is Dawn. She has been at the forefront of helping babies born into addiction, one of the biggest tragedies of the opioid epidemic.

Dawn runs Angel Arms in Latrobe, one of two nonprofits she leads while raising her own family and working on a PhD. Angel Arms has scores of "cuddlers" who care for afflicted babies and provide the love and contact that is critical to nurturing NAS babies.

One of the telltale signs of an NAS baby is a screeching, piercing cry that reflects physical pain. They're often sensitive to light and loud noises and shake uncontrollably. They may also have trouble swallowing or breathing because they didn't fully develop fully due to a mother's addiction.

This subset of babies impacted by the opioid epidemic has grown exponentially. According to the Centers for Disease Control and Prevention, NAS incidence increased 300 percent from 1999–2013 in the twenty-eight states that provided data for it. According to the Westmoreland County Children's Bureau, it received 106 referrals for drug-addicted newborns in 2017, compared to seventy-eight in 2016 and ninety-seven in 2015. Extrapolate those numbers (there are sixty-seven counties in Pennsylvania alone) and it's easy to conclude that the opioid epidemic has mass-produced the most innocent of victims.

"For a child to be born addicted to drugs is one of the most unnecessary things," Dawn said. "But it happens, so we've got to do something about it."

To Dawn, there's a difference between child abuse and an addict using drugs or alcohol while pregnant.

"An abusive parent is someone who beats their kid, and they consciously know what they're doing," she said. "A drug addict is more neglecting or trying to cope. There's no excuse for it, but it's because they're so messed up on the drug. It's not that they're not loving or good people."

Dawn has studied and worked in addiction for years, including a stint as a drug-and-alcohol counselor for Southwestern Pennsylvania Health Services. She is an unlikely person to immerse herself in addiction. She grew up in a strict Baptist household and never felt the tug of rebellion. She can, however, identify with the human condition and adversity. Dawn raised three kids after her first marriage unraveled. She worked several jobs, including cleaning houses, to support them and put herself through school.

"I was such a broken person," she said, "and I felt compassion for other (struggling) people. I asked God to heal my heart but don't ever let me forget the pain."

That led to the formation of Faith Forward in 2014. Tucked behind an old storefront on Main Street in Latrobe, it provides marriage, family and addiction counseling to those who can't afford it. The opioid epidemic blurred those lines, and Faith Forward does so much addiction-related counseling that it is recognized as an outpatient program by the Westmoreland County Drug and Alcohol Commission.

Angel Arms started shortly after Faith Forward opened when Dawn's approach to addiction—centered on action and compassion—intersected during a chance encounter.

One winter evening, a couple entered the office looking to use the phone. Dawn could see that the woman was really upset, and she talked to her. The woman was a couple of months pregnant, working as a dancer at a strip club, and mulling an abortion. Dawn forged a connection with the woman just by listening to her, and they kept in touch. When the woman was seven months pregnant, she asked Dawn if she would take her baby, so she could try to get her life together.

Dawn and her husband, Rick, agreed to it, but they had no idea what awaited them. The woman, who was so deep in addiction that she shot heroin before going to the hospital, gave birth to a son who weighed just three pounds.

Doctors weren't sure Isaac was going to live. Even after he was released from the hospital—Isaac was on morphine for a month and a half—he required constant care. He woke up every twenty minutes with a high-pitched cry, and the Hennesseys kept a close watch on his breathing since NAS babies are often born with underdeveloped lungs.

Isaac did everything later than her other kids: sit up, talk, and walk. At the age of four, he still struggled with his balance and swallowing since that reflex had yet to fully develop. He wouldn't eat some foods because of their texture and sometimes panicked when he tried swallowing.

A bigger challenge with Isaac will be keeping him away from opiates, even if he needs pain medication. Alternative medication and pain management will have to be found.

"Isaac will never remember the withdrawal, but his body will always remember the heroin," Dawn said. "If he ever needs some type of pain medication, his body will immediately snap back and remember that drug. That could turn him into another drug addict."

There isn't a lot of research when it comes to the long-term effects suffered by NAS babies. But there is hope that they will be able to overcome it with proper nurturing.

"When they did studies of crack babies in the 1980s, they found that if they got into normal housing, a loving environment, they did fine," said Dr. John Gallagher, who presides over the Pennsylvania Medical Society Opioid Task Force and has dealt extensively with expecting mothers addicted to opiates. "You'd see these babies of crack addicts who were raised in bad environments, and they did very poorly down the line. But when you took that same baby and put him into an environment where they thrived, there were no long-term problems from the crack."

Isaac's environment, in a big, loving family, will give him the chance to thrive even as he develops later than kids his age. But the Hennesseys can't take in every NAS baby. That's why Dawn created Angel Arms. Its de facto headquarters is a room inside of Faith Forward that has all the trappings of a nursery: stuffed animals and rocking chairs, a small crib and toys, a shelf filled with children's books, and a small chest with diapers and baby food.

The room is painted in cheery but not overly bright colors, and it's where Dawn's cadre of cuddlers comfort NAS babies.

They are taught to sing softly or even make clicking noises while holding the babies tightly and swaddling them. That sense of connection is critical because babies didn't get it while they developed in the womb. Dawn said NAS babies often experience the equivalent of when someone is dreaming, and they feel like they are falling. Imagine this feeling while you are awake.

"I think when you hold them, there's a security there," Dawn said.

Cuddlers get as much out of the program as the babies. Tim Sobota received a heartfelt confirmation of this when he and his wife went to Legion Keener Park in Latrobe to listen to a band. They saw the family of an NAS baby he'd cuddled. They stopped over to say hello, and Sobota didn't know if the young boy would remember him. It had, after all, been three months since he had seen him.

"He came running over and gave me the biggest hug," Sobota said. "It was really touching that he was so loving and remembered me. It really made me feel good."

An Angel Arms snuggler comforts a baby.

NAS babies sometimes bring a tear to his eye for a different reason. When we spoke, Sobota was a cuddler for Connor, a six-month-old born addicted to methadone. Connor suffers from acid reflux and stomach spasms after he eats. Connor gets so hungry that he gulps down baby food and his bottle but then starts cramping so bad that his tiny legs kick up, as if he has been punched in the stomach. The pain is so intense that Connor will cry until he is beet red in the face before exhausting himself and falling asleep. That happened the day I talked with Sobota, and Connor slept for more than an hour in his arms.

"When he woke up, he just looked up at me and gave me a big smile," Sobota said. "It's amazing the resiliency of these kids. But wow, when you see them in pain, you know there's nothing you can do except hold them and pray over them."

Sobota dealt with addiction in his own family and was looking to do volunteer work after retiring from Latrobe Steel in 2015. Angel Arms offered exactly what he coveted. He is now on the Angel Arms board of directors and said the work he does with the organization is more of a calling.

"When you give your heart to these children and you see the pain they're going through and the struggle their parents are going through, it gives you a sense of fulfillment," said Sobota, who is sixty-eight and has grandchildren of his own. "They're not asking you for anything, and you're not asking them for anything. It's about working together to make a better life for their family. If I just hold Connor through one more stomach bout and he wakes up with a big smile on his face, it's like God is answering my heart."

Carolyn Harr has developed similar connections with babies she has cuddled. One of them is one of the babies Dawn picked up while wearing her bathrobe when the grandparents needed help. Harr said he and his brother recognize her when she sees them other places. One day one of the boys blew her a kiss when his mother picked up the twins at Faith Forward. The mother said that was the first time he blew a kiss at someone.

"Do you know how much that touched my heart?" Harr said.

To Harr, it goes back to Dawn and her commitment to helping those plagued by addiction.

"She brings me to tears every time I hear her speak because her passion is contagious," Harr said, her voice cracking with emotion. "And Dawn's not going to give up. She's so determined."

Indeed, she manages to do more than most with the twenty-four hours there are in a day. Her help to mothers includes providing them with necessities, such as cribs and beds. Faith Forward has a warehouse packed with donated items for families in need, and Dawn and her staff have bigger plans to help ease the addiction problem. They want to open a restaurant and coffee house that will provide work to people trying to get back on their feet. They also want to open a youth center to provide a place for kids where they feel like they belong and get a meal if needed.

Angel Arms' most extensive project involves opening a house for mothers who have nowhere else to go. In addition to shelter, mothers will receive similar services that are now provided, albeit on a smaller scale. This includes help from cuddlers, counseling, and assistance as they rebuild their lives from the ruins of addiction.

If this seems a little ambitious for the nonprofit groups that survive on grants and donations, well, you don't know Dawn.

"How are we expecting (addicts) to change their lives if we're not helping them to do so?" Dawn said. "We're never going to get rid of this drug problem. What we little people need to do is rise up and learn how to help those we can, even if it's just one person at a time."

DOLLARS AND SENSE

Latrobe is a small city with an outsized claim to fame. It is the birthplace and home of the late Arnold Palmer, who took golf beyond the country clubs while winning eight major championships and becoming one of the most beloved sports figures of all time. Fred Rogers grew up in Latrobe, and the perpetually cheery Mr. Rogers also achieved iconic status through his eponymous TV show. The banana split was invented in Latrobe, and Rolling Rock beer was brewed there for almost sixty years. Latrobe also has the Pittsburgh Steelers, though its claim as the birthplace of professional football is not recognized by the Pro Football Hall of Fame. The six-time Super Bowl champion Steelers do spend training camp at St. Vincent College in Latrobe, a tradition that dates back more than fifty years.

Its history and natural beauty provided by mountains and rolling hills were recognized in June 2018, when Smithsonian.com named Latrobe one of the top twenty towns to visit in the United States.

There is a less idyllic side to Latrobe when you look past "Arnie's Army" and Mr. Rogers's sweaters.

Despite its charms, Latrobe has not been spared by the opioid epidemic. In 2017, ten overdose deaths occurred in the town with a population of around 8,000 people, according to the Westmoreland County

Coroner's office. That is only one less than the overdose deaths in New Kensington, whose population exceeds Latrobe's by about 5,000 people and has significant drug activity due to its economic struggles. Unity Township, which has a Latrobe mailing address, also had ten overdose deaths in 2017, according to the coroner's office, as did Derry, a neighboring township of Latrobe.

"There's something out there really bad that we've never experienced before," former Latrobe Police Chief James Bumar said.

Latrobe police officers carry Narcan, the drug that reverses overdoses. In recent years, they stopped performing tests if they seized what they suspected was heroin or some analog. It wasn't worth the exposure risk to officers if the drugs turned out to be fentanyl or carfentanil—even small contact with such potent substances can lead to sickness or worse—so they ship them to a lab where they can be handled with caution.

Bumar retired in September 2018 after spending almost thirty-five years in law enforcement, his final eight as a chief. He takes the opioid epidemic personally because he is a lifelong resident of the Latrobe area and loves his community.

"In my years of law enforcement, I have never seen a phenomenon that has such spin-off crime," Bumar told me in April 2018. "So many people arrested for heroin are involved in other crimes, and so many people you arrest for other crimes are involved with heroin. You can almost predict if you see a person stealing from their parents, doing things for money that they would (normally) never do, that they're a heroin addict."

The cost of such crime and other ripple effects from the opioid epidemic vary in different towns and cities and is difficult to quantify. In 2016, Westmoreland County performed a comprehensive review and estimated that the epidemic cost the county just under $19 million that year, almost a quarter of its budget.

"It was a little bit of an eye popper," said Rege Garris, the deputy controller who oversaw the audit. "If we get a handle on this drug problem, county expenses will go down."

The coroner's office is one place where taxpayer money could be saved. There were 174 overdose deaths in Westmoreland County in

2016. Coroner Ken Bacha estimated that every investigation of those deaths cost $3,000, based on autopsies, toxicology reports, and transportation among other expenses.

The county jail is a huge expense, Garris said, with more than 60 percent of inmates in 2016 behind bars because of drug-related crimes. There is a high recidivism rate among addicts who often go right back to the behavior that landed them in jail in the first place. That is, if they don't die from an overdose after getting out of jail because their tolerance is lower after spending time behind bars.

"It's a revolving door," Westmoreland County Commissioner Gina Cerilli said of the county prison. "You go in, you're arrested, you're released. Six months later you're back at it and back in jail."

Cerilli said overcrowding is such an issue that inmates are sometimes transferred to neighboring county prisons, assuming *they* have room.

"We have to rotate women sleeping on cots because the women's unit is full," said Cerilli, who advocates for more addiction treatment in prison. "That wasn't an issue before this drug epidemic. It's hitting women as much as it's hitting men."

Westmoreland County started a drug court in 2016 to help alleviate some of the pressure on its prison. Run by judges Meagan Bilick-DeFazio and Christopher Feliciani, addicts admitted to the program avoid jail for drug-related crimes if they follow a five-phase program that includes frequent drug testing and participation in a recovery program. It has been a positive if small step in pushing back against the opioid epidemic.

Garris, an accountant by trade, said something stirred in him when he attended the inaugural drug court graduation.

"I watched people who completed (the program) hugging the judge and thanking them for putting them on probation and shortening the leash as much as possible, so these people stayed true to it," Garris said. "I was moved by seeing people say, 'I was ready to kill myself and the best thing that happened to me was getting arrested.' I used to look at drugs more as a pure crime (issue), but now I see it as more of a condition that needs treatment."

A MOTHER'S JOURNEY

Bonnie Guldenschuh's only child showed up at her Ligonier home at 3 a.m. in tears. He had no money, no job, and nowhere to go. "Please let me in, Mom," he said in December 2015. She had kicked him out after a family friend got him into a drug and alcohol treatment center but he didn't go. She relented after she saw what looked like a skeleton wearing clothes.

Todd Guldenschuh slept most of the next two days as Bonnie mopped sweat off his brow and kept him calm through the hallucinations. They later talked for six hours, and he cried most of the time, admitting that he should have listened to her and that he'd blown everything.

But the nightmare, in some ways, was just starting for Bonnie. Like the women I met at Creekside Diner, she has been through hell because of a child's addiction. What added to her stress is she endured so much before her son fell into the clutches of heroin. She lost her mother and her husband within nine months of each other. Bonnie was also diagnosed with breast cancer during that period.

"I know it was only by the grace of God that I survived all of this," she said.

When her husband, Bill Guldenschuh, died at seventy-two after battling colon cancer, Todd was just twenty-one and had already lost of a handful of relatives.

Three months after his father died, Todd was arrested for a DUI. He completed the court requirements, but a month before his record was to be expunged, he hit a telephone pole while intoxicated. The wreck threw him from the car and into a ditch. Bonnie was able to place him into emergency psychiatric care after Todd told the police to shoot him because he didn't want to live.

"He turned into someone I didn't know," Bonnie said.

And it got worse. Much worse.

One day Todd's girlfriend called Bonnie from his apartment and told her that she couldn't wake him up. She left without calling an ambulance, and Todd's roommate came home after turning down a chance to take an extra work shift, finding Todd overdosed.

When Bonnie saw her son at Latrobe Hospital, his body was so swollen that she barely recognized him. He was on a ventilator, and doctors weren't sure he would make it through the night. They told Bonnie that there were track marks on Todd's arms.

She was in disbelief but hoped the overdose would scare him enough to go to rehab. She reached the end of her line after Todd refused to get treatment. Bonnie threw him out of the home, but he returned in tears and completely broken.

He agreed to go to Faith Farm in Fort Lauderdale, but Bonnie was about to receive her biggest scare yet. The day before Todd was scheduled to leave he met his girlfriend for coffee so he could tell her goodbye. He left in the morning and didn't arrive home until 10 p.m.

Bonnie seethed inside as she watched a Christmas movie on the Hallmark Channel. But she simply said, "Hi, honey, how are you?" as Todd walked past her and went to his bedroom. She fell asleep on the love seat and was rousted at around 3 a.m. by her dog, Bella.

"I heard a sound like a wild boar," Bonnie said, "that snorting they make before they attack something."

With Bella barking at the foot of the stairs, Bonnie realized the sound was coming from Todd's bedroom.

She raced up the stairs and burst into his room. He was flat on his back, blue and gasping for breath. She called 911 and a dispatcher told Bonnie to clear his airways. She couldn't see anything because his tongue was so swollen. The dispatcher instructed her to start CPR, so Bonnie pumped furiously on his chest while trying not to pass out herself.

She had a torn rotator cuff and the pain from performing CPR was almost unbearable. Emergency medical technicians arrived after what seemed like an eternity and reversed the overdose with a shot of Narcan. As they carried Todd out on stretcher, he had no idea what had happened.

A policewoman on the scene advised Bonnie to go to the hospital and get an EKG. But she couldn't bring herself to make that drive. She was angry. She was scared. Most of all, she was heartbroken.

She was sure that she and Bill had raised Todd right. He was a good student and active in their church. Todd was even in anti-drinking clubs at Ligonier Valley High School. His descent into drugs didn't just shock Bonnie. It pushed her to the brink.

"Looking back, there were times that I would pray at night to fall asleep and not wake up because I was just so afraid he was going to die," Bonnie said. "Something Todd once said still haunts me, and he only said it one time: 'Mom, if you've never done it and you've never gotten hooked, you can't explain it to anybody who's never done drugs.' There are still days I wake up, and he's the first thing on my mind. I still can't believe all of this happened to us."

Todd went to Faith Farm after his second near-death experience, and he successfully completed the program. He stayed in Florida, living with others in recovery. As Bonnie told me their story, she remained remarkably composed.

The one time she got emotional was when Bonnie recalled what Todd said as he pointed to her at his Faith Farm graduation ceremony: "I never, never could have made it through without that woman."

A NEW NORMAL

It didn't take much to set her off. It could be something as minor as burning dinner. It could be the crying of the baby who would never have memories of his father to call his own.

Nikki Reed was that overwhelmed after losing her husband three months earlier. Mike's death left her with two sons to raise, no income, and a gaping hole in her heart. The night Nikki really lost it came after Aiden, their older son, told her that voices were telling him to kill himself so he could be with his daddy.

She lost it in the kitchen and screamed—at God but mostly at Mike.

Are you happy? Do you see what you did to us? Your eight-year-old son has demons telling him to kill himself? I really hope that that last high was worth it.

She raged. Then she collapsed onto the floor, anger- and guilt-laced tears pouring out of her eyes.

"Everyone thinks of grief as just sadness, and it's so much more," Nikki said. "You're sad and angry, and you hate the world and everybody in it. You have moments when you're laughing at memories and everything seems okay, and the next minute you're a basket case. It's every emotion you could feel amplified by a thousand."

I talked with Nikki almost five years after her husband died at the age of thirty-three from a morphine overdose. Some of the rawness from days that were so awful that she prayed at night for God to take her persists. She and her sons don't show up in statistics that track the opioid epidemic. But their anguish amplifies how the epidemic goes beyond numbers.

"It's horrible to watch someone you love more than anything in the world deteriorate in front of your eyes and know that you can't do anything to help him," Nikki said. "If they're not sitting beside you, it's nonstop anxiety and fear. If they tell you they're going to be home at 6:00 and it's 6:15, you're ready to start calling hospitals. If my phone rang, my heart stopped. That was my life."

But Mike was the love of her life, which is why their relationship survived and sometimes thrived in spite of his addiction. They met at a party when Nikki was sixteen and each dabbled in drugs. Two years later, they were doing cocaine regularly until Nikki woke up one morning and said she was done with that part of her life. She gave birth to Aiden at the age of twenty, and Mike spent the first six months of Aiden's life on a crack cocaine binge. Money was so tight that Nikki once went a week eating nothing but Italian bread and butter, so she could buy baby formula and diapers.

The next ten years were an emotional roller coaster. Mike could be a great father, and Aiden adored him. They became extremely close and bonded over video games and fishing. But during one stretch of using, when Mike constantly left the house with friends, four-year-old Aiden asked Nikki why his daddy didn't love him anymore. Another time, after he had started injecting heroin, Mike told Nikki that he didn't love her and was only staying with her because they had a son together.

Nikki, however, stuck with him, certain that was his addiction talking. She helped get him into a treatment facility after he eventually asked for help.

Mike completed an in-patient rehab program, and he and Nikki got married. Even after Mike relapsed, he still worked and played the part of dutiful and doting husband and father. He bathed Davian, their newborn son, and spent time with Aiden. He insisted on being home for dinner. If he was running late, he always called to assure Nikki that he was okay.

"He was never the stereotypical addict that you would think of, nodding off," Nikki said. "Never took money from me, nothing like that."

The coexistence of the two Michaels didn't last. He overdosed after using morphine when he thought he was injecting heroin and died. More than 600 people crammed into a Vandergrift funeral home for his viewings. The turnout confirmed to Nikki why she loved him so much.

Aiden, also devastated by Mike's death, shut down. He stopped going outside, played video games nonstop, and barely talked to Nikki.

She gave him a notebook and told him to write what he was feeling. She assured him she would not touch it unless he wanted her to read something. One day he wrote to his father how proud he would be of Aiden for beating the latest edition of Call of Duty, a popular video game they often played together, the last time two days before Mike died.

Troubling signs soon emerged. Aiden started getting into fights and lashing out in anger. He almost burned the house down after he started a fire in his bedroom. What disturbed Nikki most about the incident was that he didn't call for help. Had she been asleep and not smelled the smoke, she never would have reached Aiden in time.

Desperate to help Aiden, she enrolled him in therapy, and he was diagnosed with extreme post-traumatic stress disorder (PTSD). Almost five years after the loss of his father, he still has anger issues, and Nikki worries about the long-term effect Michael's death will have on their first-born son. Sometimes she sees Aiden in his bedroom, holding a picture of his father. She knows by looking at Aiden whether to leave him alone or wrap her arms around him and cry with him.

"I miss him, too," she said. "Every day."

Davian also misses his father even though he never knew him. Nikki often finds him looking at pictures of Mike and crying. One time a babysitter overheard Davian telling other kids that his dad was in heaven, and they were lucky that they have fathers. The babysitter was in tears when she told Nikki the story.

It took Nikki almost four years, but she opened up to another serious relationship. After more than six months of dating, Nikki and her boyfriend moved in together. He is great with her kids and respectful of the situation. He bought a cabinet for the living room to display pictures of Mike and the urn holding Mike's ashes. He understands why Nikki still wears her wedding rings and if he proposes? Well, they will deal with that when it happens.

Of more immediate concern to Nikki is when her sons lash out at him for no reason other than that he isn't their father. She said Davian tells her he loves her boyfriend but will later act as if he is trying to drive him away. When he was put in his bedroom after misbehaving one time, he slammed into the door until it came off the hinges.

It was another reminder to Nikki that life without Mike is a work in progress. But at least Nikki can see that life. For the longest time she couldn't. She and Mike were together for half of her life, and a part of her died with him.

"It took me a long time to get here and not go through the motions of my day," she said. "I found myself and I can actually live my life. I can laugh now, and it's actually real."

ADDICTION AND RECOVERY

He gave his testimony at a New Year's Eve party that featured a band playing gospel music. He spent the last hour of 2017, walking with a group from Covenant Christian Ministries to the Westmoreland County Courthouse. They passed New Year's Eve revelers along the way, and what was no more than a half-mile walk in downtown Greensburg seemed like miles.

Temperatures hovered in single digits. A lashing wind made it even colder. Snow covered the sidewalks, making it difficult to wheel an enormous wooden cross covered with the names of people who fatally overdosed to the Courthouse. But the group endured, carried by the same sense of purpose and spirit that infused the party that had served nothing harder than soda.

Shortly before midnight, candles were lit and a brief service was held in the otherwise quiet Courthouse square.

I stood next to thirty-four-year-old Greg Powell, who was twenty months clean when I first met him. He uses a cane to help with his balance, and when I mentioned how bitterly cold it was, he smiled. It was nothing, he said, compared to when he slept in his car or inside of a Wal-Mart because he had nowhere else to go.

Greg shows that there *is* hope from the despair of addiction. His story is also emblematic of how nothing seems to make any sense about the opioid epidemic. The reason: it took a catastrophic accident to save his life. If that sounds dramatic consider that Greg, who spent roughly half of his life in addiction, has not battled urges to use since getting hit by a train on April 22, 2016 in Westmoreland City. Juxtapose that with his earlier life and it is stunning.

Greg robbed drug dealers and was shot at by them. He once sped away from an accident because he had drugs and a gun in his car only to encounter a police roadblock with guns pointed at him. He endured the hell of withdrawal in an overcrowded holding area, writhing in pain on a prison floor with just one toilet to share with scores of others going through the same thing.

"I thought I was going to die a heroin addict," Greg said. "I'm pretty sure my family thought I was going to die an addict as well. I felt like a puppet, like somebody else was pulling my strings."

That loss of control to addiction led to Greg spending almost four years in jail just for probation violations. He attended more than thirty funerals in his twenties and early thirties. And most of the deaths were drug related, including one that took place on the train tracks near his house.

It involved a man Greg had become good friends through Narcotics Anonymous. They started going to church together and became so close that the man's young son referred to Greg as his uncle. The man relapsed after a year of sobriety and bought heroin. Greg planned to meet him but first stopped at a convenience store. When he got to the train tracks, he found his friend dead of an overdose.

Finding his friend wasn't even the worst death he associates with train tracks. His younger brother and one of his best friends were hit by a train and killed. Against this backdrop, Greg embarked on a walk along the train tracks to a friend's house—a walk that almost cost him his life and may have ultimately saved it. He took the tracks because it was more a direct shot to his friend's house and a good way to avoid his probation officer. He stopped near a creek to think and doesn't remember crossing the train tracks after he started walking again.

"I woke up three months later," Greg said.

His brain was so scrambled that Greg spoke "jibberish" when he emerged from the coma. He thought he was French. He needed twenty head surgeries and seventy percent of his skull is comprised of titanium rods. One of the plates in his head was inserted to keep brain matter from seeping into his sinus cavity. In the first two years after his accident, Greg spent more days in the hospital than at home. Five times doctors asked him to designate someone power of attorney prior to surgery.

When I asked him how he even survived getting hit by a train, Greg smiled.

"I've heard the words *anomaly* and *miracle* many times from doctors," he said. "If you didn't believe in God before you met me, you're a fool not to now. The day I was hit by the train, I was freed from all my addictions."

Greg Powell (right) talks with Kevin Stevens before
a panel discussion on the opioid epidemic.

Greg credits his faith with keeping him free.

"That's the only thing that worked for me," he said. "I couldn't have done it without Jesus."

Greg had tried everything else to get clean. He was in and out of rehab for years. Methadone, a narcotic that is used to wean people off heroin, proved to be more addictive for Greg than heroin. Suboxone, a narcotic that blocks the brain receptors that crave opiates, helped Greg keep a construction job and maintain a relatively normal lifestyle. But Greg never truly felt free from addiction until he fully committed to his religion.

He attends church and Bible studies regularly. He also takes part in Greater Things, a Greensburg-based group that incorporates religion into its recovery program and gives back by feeding the homeless.

"If it wasn't for my relationship with Jesus and being a born-again Christian, I wouldn't be clean right now," Greg said. "I credit it all to Him because I couldn't do it by myself for all those years. I've been through NA and AA. I've been to over twenty rehabs. I didn't get clean until I completely surrendered to Jesus. It's hard to tell people that because some people don't want to hear that or don't believe that."

As for the catastrophic accident that may have just saved his life, Greg said, "I don't want to give the train too much credit, but something the enemy was trying to use to take me out God turned around and used to change my life. I almost forget what it was like when I was an addict. It's like the reset button has been hit."

WHY STIGMA STINGS

A PROMISE TO CASEY

She arrived at an Applebee's restaurant in Pittsburgh, still in the scrubs she wears as a radiology technologist at Allegheny General Hospital.

It wasn't long after we were seated that Michelle Schwartzmier tried to put me at ease.

"You can't say the wrong thing. You can't hurt me more than I've already been hurt," she said.

Almost a year since Michelle lost her daughter, Casey, she had emerged as a symbol of transparency, the antidote to a disease that thrives in darkness. It all started with a promise that Michelle hoped she would never have to keep. Casey battled addiction since her teenage years and once showed Michelle an obituary for someone who died of an overdose. The obituary spoke to Casey because of its candor, and she said it made her feel a little less lonely in her addiction. She wanted to do the same for others if something happened to her.

Michelle had never imagined she would talk about Casey's obituary with her only daughter.

They were the typical suburban family with Michelle and her husband, Richard, involved in both of their kids' activities. Casey loved to sing and dance, and she became a cheerleader and a competitive dancer. She had a great high kick in Tae Kwon Do and needed only two years of training to earn a black belt. Her brother, Eric, played baseball and also earned a black belt in Tae Kwon Do.

The family bonded during camping trips and huddled around the TV for Steelers games. They also welcomed several additions to the family because of Casey's love of animals. She saved a black cat named London after she heard he was going to be euthanized. Michelle probably would have given in had Casey simply asked if they could take in London. But Casey sealed the deal by making a power-point presentation on why the family needed another pet.

That was Casey.

Like many teenagers, Casey experimented, and her parents responded accordingly. They grounded her and took away her cell phone when she got caught with beer at a slumber party at the age of fourteen. What they thought was typical teenage behavior quickly escalated, and Casey came to her mother in tears one day. She confessed that she had started taking pills and couldn't stop. Another time Michelle got a text message from Casey's ex-boyfriend that Casey was going to try heroin. Michelle confronted her, and Casey admitted that she was using heroin.

Her parents got her counseling and treatment, and Casey had been in and out of several in-patient rehabilitation centers by the time she came across the obituary she shared with Michelle. It had been a time of real hope as Casey was set to leave for a treatment center in California, determined to reclaim her life from heroin. She and Michelle had some deep conversations. When Casey asked her to write an honest obituary if she died, Michelle asked her if she was sure.

"Tell them my story," Casey told her. "If it can help just one person, it's worth it."

*   *   *

Michelle is brutally honest when she tells Casey's story—whether it is to one person or a high school auditorium filled with kids she wants to save. *Casey was you.*

That is her message. It is an uncomfortable truth delivered poignantly from a grieving mother. And it always flows from the heart since Michelle never speaks with note cards.

Terry Struble, the superintendent of Clearfield School District in central Pennsylvania, heard Michelle at a reality tour in Westmoreland County and arranged for her to speak to his students.

She told Casey's story to more than one thousand kids that day. She took vacation days from work to speak, and Struble had to insist that the school put her up in a hotel for two nights. Michelle made such an impact that the students wanted to continue the discussion she started when they returned to class. One teacher emailed Michelle to tell her that students were still talking about the speech a week later.

"She is absolutely amazing and takes no pay," Struble said. "If we get someone off the national circuit, we're spending $2,000 to $3,000—and that's if we can split that with another school district."

Michelle never intended to become a sought-after speaker, but it all started when she posted the obituary she wrote to her Facebook page:

> Casey Marie Schwartzmier, age 20, passed away on Sunday, January 15, 2017, of an accidental heroin overdose after a long brave battle with addiction. She is survived by her parents, Richard and Michelle (Waldorf) Schwartzmier, her brother Eric Schwartzmier, grandparents Mary (Planic) and the late Richard F. Schwartzmier, Jerome B. Waldorf, and many aunts, uncles and cousins. Casey never wanted to be defined only by her addiction and mistakes, she was so much more than that. She made it clear if she was to ever pass as a result of it, she wanted people to know the truth with the hope that honesty about her death could help break the stigma about addicts and get people talking about the problem of addiction that is taking away so many young lives.
>
> Casey was a beautiful, intelligent child of the suburbs who fell into its grip. It can happen to anyone. She was feisty and outspoken but would do anything for anyone and always lit up the room with her smile and sense of humor, even while struggling with her demons. She loved her family deeply, wanted to adopt every animal she saw, and play with every child she came across. Casey believed strongly in second

chances, maybe because she craved another chance for herself and other addicts, so she donated her life-saving organs to give someone else a second chance at life. That was Casey . . . this amazing woman should be remembered for this and not her mistakes. Casey believed that hiding her cause of death would help no one, but if her story could help just one addict push even harder for another day of sobriety, encourage an active user to choose recovery, or shine a light on this horrible epidemic, then it would be worth coming out of the shadows. She was very open about her struggles and now is not the time to change that.

This strong attitude with a fierce drive and loving, beautiful heart that wanted to help other addicts even in death is one of the many things that she can be defined by, not her addiction. Casey wanted to live. She had dreams of a future career and children of her own, and fought hard all the way until the end, one day away from entering rehab, but couldn't break the chains of this demon that's wiping out a generation. Addiction doesn't discriminate, it will take hold and destroy anyone in its path, including the families and people who love them. Addiction hides in the faces of everyday people all around us. Casey isn't just another statistic or just "another one gone too soon," she was a great heart with a bright future and a gift that the world lost and can never be replaced. So the best way to honor Casey is for people who read this or knew her to think twice before you judge an addict.

The obituary spread on social media at breakneck speed. One day a Pittsburgh TV station called and asked Michelle if she knew that Casey's obituary had gone viral. She started receiving messages from all over the world, some from addicts thanking her for speaking out.

She went online to look for articles about Casey and found a few in languages she doesn't speak.

The day the Steelers played the New England Patriots in the 2017 AFC Championship Game and two days after the inauguration of a new president, Casey's story was on the front page of the *Pittsburgh Post-Gazette*. Casey would have gotten a kick out of that, and Michelle said to her son, Eric, "Your sister trumped Trump."

In early February, Eric sent Michelle a text message that read, "Um, the White House just called. You should probably call them back."

Eric had Googled the area code that had been left on the family answering machine, and it was indeed for Washington DC. Michelle called the number given to her for the office of the National Drug Control Policy and was told, "Casey's story has reached the White House, and we're listening."

* * *

Casey Schwartzmier. Photo courtesy of Michelle Schwartzmier.

Michelle won't stop speaking out even though she sometimes struggles with one of the messages she preaches.

"Parents need to know they didn't do anything wrong," Michelle said. "That's so hard for me because I can say it to somebody else, but trying to believe it myself is hard because I question the same things they do. It's not their fault but I still have to try to convince myself of that. I think about every little thing that happened in her life. When she was four years old, did I yell at her? Should I have gone to a different rehab to get her help? Should I have gotten her treatment sooner? I just question a million things, and it's never ending."

One of the questions Michelle struggles with involves the larger issue of treatment—and the difficulty addicts and their families can encounter due to issues ranging from insurance to a general shortage of facilities. Casey was scheduled to go to treatment earlier, but the center where they reserved a bed wouldn't take Michelle's insurance after it changed at the start of the new year. They found a new place, but it took almost two weeks. Michelle and her family will never know if Casey would still be alive had she gone to treatment earlier.

The night before Casey was to fly to California, she overdosed at home. Paramedics rushed Casey to the hospital where Michelle works. When some of her colleagues saw Michelle, they thought she was at the hospital for work, not realizing that the overdose that came in was her daughter. Casey fought for five days in the hospital before dying, something her mother attributes to her spirit and her will to live.

A toxicology report later showed that Casey died from a fentanyl overdose. Fentanyl is a synthetic form of heroin and much more potent than heroin. What makes it so lethal is someone may take it not knowing if it's straight fentanyl or heroin cut with fentanyl.

"I go home every day to where she overdosed, and I go to work every day to where she died," Michelle said, her voice catching with emotion. "It really is pretty horrible. It's hard to speak about it, but I keep doing it because I know it has to be done. I want to stay in bed a lot of days, and I cry every day."

She paused and said, "There are now two Michelles. There's Michelle who's become an advocate trying to save someone else's child. Then there's Casey's mom who's just really sad. They're both me. It's just which role I play each day or minute."

The willingness to speak out is something Casey inspired even before she talked to Michelle about her obituary. Casey was always outspoken and candid about her addiction. Michelle's colleague once sent Casey a friend request on Facebook, and Casey asked Michelle if it was okay to accept it. Michelle said she didn't have a problem with it but that she had generally refrained from talking about her addiction to protect Casey's privacy.

Given her work in a hospital emergency room, it is easy to see why Michelle might have been uncomfortable talking about Casey's struggles.

"You're on the frontlines in the ER, and you get frustrated because a guy has been here ten times in the last couple of weeks (from an overdose)," she said. "People would say dismissive things like, 'That junkie in the corner,' and they didn't realize they were talking about my daughter as far as I was concerned. A lot of people are going through what I did, and when other people make horrible comments, they don't realize who they're talking to because addiction is this dirty little secret you're not allowed to talk about."

Her determination to shine a light on it has turned into a second job. Michelle speaks so often in Westmoreland County that advocates joke she is now an honorary resident. She also answers every message she receives on Facebook, no matter how late it is.

"It's heartbreaking because I've had some addicts who reached out to me who were very encouraged by Casey's obituary, and some of them have died since then," she said. "I think, 'Wow am I really helping?' Then I get another message from someone else that says I am helping, so I just try to focus on that. Casey connected with a transparent obituary, so apparently other addicts do, too."

Michelle and I spoke for more than an hour that night. She talked glowingly about her son and how he planned to study actuary sciences in college. She said with a laugh that she had to look up the major that deals with numbers and probabilities because she had never heard of it. She talked with anguish about the complications Casey endured after a tonsillectomy when she was thirteen years old. She suffered severe bleeding and required a second surgery. She was prescribed Vicodin for the pain, and Michelle said she followed the doctor's instructions carefully in giving Casey the pain medication. Had that somehow set her on a deadly collision course with heroin?

Such questions are normal for a parent grieving the loss of a child and pondering what could have been done differently. I couldn't help but wonder about the tangle and intensity of emotions Michelle would deal with over the next month. Her first Christmas without Casey was in less than two weeks. The first anniversary of Casey's death was less than a month after that.

But Michelle doesn't miss Casey any less on a regular Wednesday than a holiday. And her profound sense of loss is triggered by the most mundane things. When she goes to a supermarket, she thinks about what Casey would have bought. When she looks at a restaurant menu, she wonders what Casey would have ordered.

"That's what I go through all day, every day," Michelle said.

SOCIETY IS NOT SENSITIVE

Dr. Jonathan Han has spent his career working in community medicine and in areas that are underserved. His practice is in New Kensington in the northern part of Westmoreland County, and it has been proactive in dealing with the opioid epidemic.

It prescribes Suboxone and Vivitrol—both block opioid receptors—while two addiction specialists in the office provide counseling, a critical component of medical-assisted treatment. Han's New Kensington practice also distributes Narcan.

This is the second epidemic in which Han has found himself on the forefront. He worked as a medical resident in San Francisco when the AIDS epidemic gripped the United States, and those afflicted with the disease were shunned and scorned because of perceived moral failings.

Han said what is happening now with addicts is "completely comparable" to the AIDS epidemic "because there was so much stigma and hatred. The same thing happened with HIV because it was a marginalized population at the time, mostly gay men who everyone felt comfortable hating on in public."

What makes stigma particularly counterproductive now is that it can keep addicts and their family members in the shadows and discourage them from getting help.

"Nothing else is going to change until we fix the stigma," said Ashley Rudnik, who worked as a nurse at UPMC East in Monroeville before taking a similar job at a hospital in Morgantown, West Virginia. "I see it every day. When we get beeped with an admission coming, many times the nurse will get the paperwork and the eyes roll, like, 'Oh great, another drug addict. Another junkie.' That's the attitude nurses have, and we are supposed to be the most compassionate people. So, what is everybody else thinking?"

Ashley, a recovering addict, has seen it from both sides.

She battled a heroin problem so severe that only a botched injection of the same drug that killed pop singer Michael Jackson saved her life. It happened after she failed a drug test at work. She lost her job on the spot but was allowed to drive home. She wrecked twice on the way to her apartment. After the second accident, she fell asleep in her car while waiting for the police to arrive. She managed to talk her way out of more serious trouble by telling police that she had just worked a sixteen-hour shift at the hospital and was simply exhausted.

Her instinct for self-preservation had all but evaporated by the time Ashley got home. She took Propofol, an anesthetic used to stop breathing. She called her mother and told her about the suicide attempt, and her mother called 911. When firefighters broke into her apartment, they found her naked and covered in blood. The IV she had stuck in her arm dislodged after she lost consciousness. That is the only thing that saved her life.

Ashley told me this near-death story a day before her thirtieth birthday. More than four years into her recovery, she had regained her nursing license through the Pennsylvania Nursing Assistance Program and become a member of its board.

The former Greensburg resident is open about her story to remind herself where she had once been and to encourage others battling addiction. But Ashley knows why others, even those in recovery, may be hesitant when it comes to transparency. She cited a fellow nurse, who had also been an addict and stolen drugs from work. That nurse told her story on a Pittsburgh TV station. But even with the anonymity given to her (the station didn't show her face during the interview), she might have second-guessed the decision, based on the reaction to her interview.

The story was posted to the station's Facebook page, and Ashley said most of the comments were "atrocious." Some told the woman she had disgraced her profession. Others called her a junkie and said should just overdose and die. Never mind that the woman was in recovery.

"For every comment that praised this woman for making her life better, there were ten comments that told her to go kill herself," Ashley said.

Such vitriol would not surprise Mike Baacke.

Like Ashley, he extricated himself from the grip of addiction and is a shining example in the recovery community. Mike started with nothing after getting out of a treatment facility in 2011. He lived in a trailer and worked odd jobs on weekends just to pay rent. He finally got enough money from a tax return to buy a truck. He eventually built a successful roofing and contracting business. Mike restores and flips houses and hopes to one day own enough apartment buildings and properties to turn them over to someone else to manage.

He takes his recovery as seriously as his work and almost never misses a weekly Narcotics Anonymous meeting. He used to tell his story during reality tours, which give students a sobering look at where addiction leads. But he stopped doing that when he became a business owner.

"I didn't want the stigma put on me," Mike said. "If I'm standing up there saying, 'Hey I used to steal and shoot heroin' and you call to get a roof estimate and I knock on your door, I'm the guy that was the drug addict. I'm not putting my face on it because then it affects my kids eating. I think after a certain amount of time, I'll be comfortable with it, (but) society is not a sensitive place."

Mike gives back in another way by hiring people in recovery and helping them with loans or in other areas where they may have nowhere else to turn because of their past. He protects himself by only hiring people with at least six months of recovery, so he knows they're serious about it. He also makes it clear that he will help his employees if they relapse but only if they are honest with him. As a former addict, he can detect the telltale signs of using and manipulation.

"People can get better," Mike said. "But there's no compassion. There's no empathy. It has to change. It's hard to sit back and watch society's view on addicts because they're like, 'Oh, let them die.' I've been there."

Han said human decency needs to prevail to combat such attitudes—and stigma in general.

"The problem is when we have this attitude where it's sort of like,' Oh, you're an addict because you're lazy,'" Han said. "That feeling is so pervasive, and that bias is so strong. It's important for people to analyze their sense of judgment. When we start devaluing people, that's when we head down the road to hell."

Such devaluing manifests itself in more ways than just how society views addicts. Consider treatment itself. If someone suffers a heart attack, they aren't told to return to the hospital when there is a bed available. Yet all too often an addict seeking treatment is told just that. That approach may be symptomatic of a larger issue, that despite a medical consensus that addiction is a disease, it isn't treated as such. A lot of that goes back to stigma.

"What other disease do we wait for it to get worse before we do anything?" said Rich Jones, a Westmoreland County native who heads the outreach program Faces and Voices of Recovery in South Carolina. "It's the equivalent of going to your oncologist and they say, 'You've got stage one cancer, but we're going to wait until it hits stage five' before it is treated."

Bishop Edward Malesic, one of the top religious leaders in Westmoreland County, asserts that addiction should be treated like a disease, not dismissed as a moral failing. Malesic, head of the Roman Catholic Diocese of Greensburg, formed a task force in 2016 after he had "heard enough" about the opioid epidemic. The ad hoc committee staged seven sessions throughout the area in 2017 that provided a mixture of prayer and education for those in need. He told me about one exchange after a session in Kittanning that stayed with him long after it happened.

It was with a man and woman who attended a session with their two grandchildren. Their son missed most of the session because he attended a 12-step meeting, but he was with his parents later when they asked Malesic to pray for him. The young man died three days later. Two weeks later, Malesic received a letter from the man's parents. They thanked him for praying for their son that night and said he had a look of peace after they prayed. It was a sharp contrast to what they saw during his battle with addiction.

Such interactions personalize addiction for Malesic. They also reinforce to him how strong a grip that opioids have on addicts.

"For them, it's not a choice not to do it," he said. "They would like to stop, but their body tells them they can't. Then they'll get into that mode of, 'I'm not lovable because I'm a drug addict. I've hurt my parents and my parents are embarrassed, so they would never love me.' Then they begin to realize how much has been taken from them. Then it's like, 'I'm going to die anyway.'"

It is a deadly cycle, perpetuated by shame and despair. Stopping it is tied to shattering stigma. One way to do that is to refrain from viewing someone simply in the context of addiction.

STIGMA WITHIN STIGMA

All Austin Hixson has to do to realize how lucky he was to recover from a heroin addiction is leaf through one of his old yearbooks. Austin graduated from Yough High School in 2007 and said at least fifteen people from his class have died from overdoses. He is the only one who is both alive and not in prison among his five closest friends from high school. His two best friends died of overdoses, as did his next-door neighbor.

"When my core group started using heroin, it was still sort of (taboo)," Austin said. "I went away to college, and two years later I'm back, and *everybody* is doing it. People I would never imagine were doing it. It exploded like a bomb."

The numbing loss that unfolded around him makes it all the more perplexing to Austin that he usually feels the need to add this qualifier when saying he is on methadone: he plans to get off it soon.

Never mind that he has been taking methadone for more than seven years—and during that time has become a certified recovery specialist for Southwestern Pennsylvania Health Services in Greensburg and got married. Austin has freed himself from addiction but not quite the stigma that comes with it.

"I don't know why pressure is put on people (to get off methadone)," he said. "Some people want to get off it, and that's fantastic. Use it for however it works for you. It saved my life."

The controversy stirred by methadone—and the stigma it stokes— stems from the fact that it's an opiate, though one that has proven effective when taken in concert with counseling. It is part of the medical-assisted treatment approach to opiate addiction and includes Suboxone, Vivitrol, and Revia. The four either block opiate receptors or take away cravings for opiates.

Methadone is a lightning rod for critics who claim that because it is an opiate, taking it merely kicks the can of addiction down the road. It adds another layer to the complexity of the opioid epidemic because of the additional stigma those on medical-assisted treatment face.

"There is nothing that has more misinformation than methadone," said Austin, who meticulously studied medical-assisted treatment before entering recovery. "The recovery community is one of the hardest places to change minds."

Medical-assisted treatment is generally rejected by 12-step programs such as Narcotics Anonymous because a chemical element is part of its recovery.

"A lot of our people on medical-assisted treatment tell us that they don't like going to NA meetings because a lot of people discount it. They see it as still using drugs," Han said. "There's a lot of stigma about what is considered clean or not."

It would be harder to find someone more fed up with the stigma that envelops medical-assisted treatment than Kelley Lord.

Lord is a counselor at Medmark, a methadone and Suboxone clinic in Greensburg. She said her pleas to be heard about the potential benefits of medical-assisted treatment largely meet closed minds when she reaches out to people on the front lines of the opioid epidemic.

"I have tried to be a voice since I started here, but I'm seen as the seedy counselor because I work in the seedy facility," said Lord, who has been at Medmark since 2016 and was named BayMark Health Services Clinician of the Year in 2017. "I'm seeing monumental changes in people and I can't stand that they feel bad for coming here amongst everything else they are dealing with. There is no cookie-cutter way to recovery. What does it matter what route (addicts) choose for help as long as they get there? I don't get it."

Lord unwittingly conducted an experiment in April 2018, when her frustration reached a tipping point. She and her husband spent a Saturday afternoon planting signs in Greensburg and Youngwood that provided a phone number for those interested in methadone or Suboxone. The signs were simple and placed in public areas among a cluster of other signs.

Lord said they posted around forty signs. Two weeks later, only one of them was still standing.

"It tells me that everyone in these different areas have that same opinion: get the signs out of here," Lord said. "I want to put up another sign that says, 'Would you rather have (addicts) steal, break into your car, rob your house or would you rather have them try treatment?' But *you*, for whatever reason, don't agree with methadone or Suboxone, so you're going to take away an opportunity (at recovery). It was very disheartening."

Katrin Schall would not be surprised by such a story. Kat is a certified recovery specialist for Southwestern Pennsylvania Health Services in Greensburg and is nothing if not transparent about her past.

"My rap sheet is twenty-one pages long," the former heroin addict said. "You name it, I did it. In and out of jail from the time I was eighteen until I was thirty-one."

She has been clean for more than seven years and is a leader in the recovery community. Her work includes teaching life skills and recovery at the Westmoreland County Prison. She recalled the surreal feeling of returning there for the first time after she started working in recovery. A part of her wanted to make sure they would let her back out when she was finished with her session.

Kat credits her sobriety to turning her life over to Jesus Christ and said she never succeeded with medical-assisted treatment. Kat, however, admitted that her motives weren't pure when she tried methadone. She advocates for any path to recovery. That includes needle exchanges as well as shooting galleries for addicts. The goal is to keep addicts alive, so an opening can be found to get them into treatment. Not that Kat holds out hope that programs such as needle exchanges will make their way to Westmoreland County because of stigma.

"Do you think that the public is going to allow it? Never," Kat said. "People are naïve. They don't think it's in their backyard. It's in your front yard. It's in your kids' schools. My daughter is twenty, and she graduated two years ago from Latrobe High School, and kids were shooting up on the bus."

* * *

Medmark's location is symbolic of methadone's standing in society. It's housed in a large, white building that is tucked away from the back roads that run past it. The clinic is in the back of the building and can be hard to find even from the parking lot. The stigma that Kelley Lord hears about doesn't just happen outside of Medmark's clinic.

One of her clients told her his probation officer all but ordered him to get off methadone despite his staying out of trouble while on it. Another client told her how happy his mother is that he is not using heroin but that she would stop talking to him if she knew he was on methadone. Other Lord clients tell family members they are going to the gym when they are going to Medmark for their methadone dose.

Lord said such secrecy can compromise the therapy component of medical-assisted treatment since it runs counter to transparency.

What is telling about the medical-assisted treatment disconnect is that it is largely endorsed by the medical community. That includes Dr. John Gallagher, who chairs the Pennsylvania Medical Society Opioid Task Force.

"Our argument is if somebody is on insulin for diabetes, we don't try to wean them off," he said. "If we get somebody on methadone and Suboxone, and by using other programs, we eventually get them off it, wonderful. But people who are addicted to medication will do anything to avoid withdrawal (even) if that means selling their kids, robbing a bank, or taking money from their mother. When they're on methadone, they avoid withdrawal and have a normal lifestyle. They can function, so now they can get jobs, keep their jobs, and take care of their family. What's wrong with that?"

That is the question that makes Lord want to pull her hair out.

Ask her about some of the methadone criticism, and she has an answer. Is it a moneymaker? Even if it is, Lord said, so is medication to treat bipolar disorder, and people who take medicine for that are praised. Can someone overdose on methadone? Yes, Lord said, but nothing is fool-proof, and the program is strict and regimented when done properly. Is it a crutch? Yes, Lord said, but if you break your leg, you aren't expected to walk on your own right away. They call them crutches for a reason.

Ultimately, Lord doesn't see her pushing medical-assisted treatment as much as embracing possible solutions to the opioid epidemic.

"It's whatever treatment someone can find that works because we are in a pandemic," she said. "What we've been doing isn't working. We need to try something else."

Austin Hixson can't understand the fuss over something that takes a fraction of his week. He takes a dose of methadone every day, as someone might take a pill for hypertension, and he stops at Medmark once a week to pick up his doses. He achieved that level of oversight by successfully completing a program that includes counseling and drug testing and gradually grants more freedom to those who advance in it.

"There will be a time I come off methadone," Austin said. He paused and added, "I think."

That is also the long-term goal of Howie Boelky.

I met with the Irwin resident the day he helped with a Medmark orientation session, and he attributed his yearlong sobriety to more than just a daily dose of methadone. Howie's story shows how medical-assisted treatment works if a person is committed to recovery, following the program, and dealing with the consequences if they falter.

Howie initially griped about having to go to the clinic every day for his medicine. During early counseling sessions, he was *that* guy who made snide remarks and showed no interest in participating. That masked his reluctance to be honest with himself and share his story because of shame.

Howie, who is thirty-eight, started drinking and smoking marijuana at an early age to escape a dysfunctional household. That escalated to crack cocaine, and he tried heroin for the first time when he was nineteen. He got clean during a stint in prison and built a life for himself after he got out of jail. Howie got married, and he and his wife had two sons. He started a contracting and roofing business.

His business and marriage crashed after Howie relapsed. He had been clean four years when he hurt his back on the job and started buying pain pills on the street. He started using heroin again. Before long, he was stealing copper from abandoned houses to pay for his habit. He lost everything and tried to intentionally overdose one Christmas Eve. He woke up the next day and turned himself in on several outstanding warrants.

Opening up about a one-time fifty-bag-a-day heroin habit, he also shared that the eighteen months he once spent in Westmoreland County Prison passed without one visit, phone call, or letter from any family member: That is how fed up they were with him. It's hard for Howie to relive his past, and he got emotional at times while talking about it.

"I try to bury all of that stuff," he said. "I was a dirtbag. That's the life I had."

The big blue eyes he sees staring back at him every day are all the reasons he needs to continue with the life he has now. Howie is remarried and has two daughters: Riley, five, and Emma, three.

"They melt my heart," he said. "When I see them, it makes me power on and do what I have to do to provide a life for them that I didn't have."

When we met, Howie had completed enough steps in the methadone program that he was only a couple of months away from having his visits to Medmark reduced to two times a week. He didn't want to stop there.

"Until I'm off the methadone, I'm not completely sober. I'm in recovery," he said. "My goal is to be completely clean when I get out of the program. Some people stay in the methadone clinic their entire lives. Good for them. They're off the dope. They're clean, they're working, and they're doing what they need to do. If they have to come here and get one milligram of methadone for the rest of their lives, great."

THEY'RE HUMAN BEINGS

Her presentations usually include a scenario in which someone is lying unconscious on a sidewalk and needs Narcan. She asks the audience to create that person in their mind. Is it a male or female? How old are they? Are they married? Do they have kids? What do they do for a living? Do they live in a house or an apartment? What is their socio-economic status?

She then pivots to a 911 dispatcher getting a call about this person, and it isn't his or her first overdose. She finally asks the audience how many times that person should receive Narcan.

"I usually get between the number one and seven," Christine Ackerman said. "Then I say, 'My name is Christine and I am that addict. I was Narcaned six times.'"

Christine had been in recovery for more than two years when she told me about the exercise that measures public opinion on Narcan. She speaks freely about her fentanyl addiction and making it through to the other side. Christine also volunteers more than thirty hours a week at Sage's Army in Irwin, and most of that time is spent working the organization's hotline.

Addicts or their family members call the hotline, and Sage's Army places them in treatment. It sounds simple; it is anything but that. Calls are made to locate a facility with an open bed and one that accepts the insurance of the person in need of treatment. It can be daunting for someone who is already beaten down, and Christine offers a calming presence as well as empathy that comes easily based on her own experience. Few calls gave her more satisfaction than one she received in December 2017 from a heroin addict in Baltimore.

The man's family lived in Johnstown, which is how he knew about Sage's Army. He was living out of his car with nothing, including hope. Christine talked to him about his situation and arranged for his mother to prepay for fuel at a nearby gas station, so he could drive back to Western Pennsylvania. She also arranged for him to stay at a men's shelter in Latrobe until a bed opened at Pyramid Healthcare in Wilkinsburg.

Her work didn't end there. Christine talked with the man for almost four hours as he drove from Baltimore to Latrobe. He arrived safely at the shelter, spent ninety days at Pyramid, and moved to Washington County after completing inpatient treatment. When the man celebrated six months of sobriety at a Narcotics Anonymous meeting, Christine was there to hug him as if he had returned from the dead—which he essentially had.

What makes her story unique is ten years earlier, Christine would have given this number had someone asked how many times a person should receive Narcan: *zero.*

Yes, zero.

"I hated addicts," she said. "Hated them. I adamantly believed that addiction was a choice."

She viewed addiction through the prism of someone who put herself through school despite having three kids by the age of twenty-two and built a successful career in nursing. In her mind, addiction was not a disease; it was simply people making bad decisions.

That sentiment crystallized in the summer of 2008, while Christine and a friend were walking from Children's Hospital in Pittsburgh to nearby Presbyterian Hospital. During the short walk, Christine, who worked nights at Children's Hospital as a trauma nurse, saw a man go ballistic outside of the Presbyterian Hospital emergency room.

From his yelling, she figured that the hospital had refused to refill a subscription. Christine guessed it was narcotics because who loses their mind over not getting more amoxicillin? The man started throwing orange construction barrels, and security tackled and subdued him. The scene infuriated Christine, especially considering what she saw every day at work.

She worked with children battling cancer—Christine sometimes wore SpongeBob SquarePants scrubs to help take the kids' minds off their daily struggle—and comforted parents who prayed they would live. Here was someone acting like an unhinged brat because he couldn't get a prescription refilled? Who in the hell did he think he was?

Christine said to her friend, "I hate junkies. We should shoot them in the head. They don't recover."

A year later a serious car accident started her down the path of addiction.

She was hit coming home from work one night after a car driven by a nun crossed into her lane. Paramedics had to cut Christine out of her car before she was life-flighted to Presbyterian Hospital. In a cruel twist, the helicopter landed at Children's Hospital because it shared a helipad with Presby. Christine aspired be a flight nurse and ride in emergency helicopters, such as the one that dropped her at the helipad as an accident victim.

The car crash left her with a broken back and pelvis. It also caused enough brain trauma that Christine forgot how to count and could only read her own writing. A month into her recovery she achieved a breakthrough when she was able to count to fifteen. Christine later had fourteen rods inserted in her body to stabilize her back. By then, pain management was a persistent issue in her life.

"One prescription became another became another became another," Christine said.

She abused her pain medication to the point that she no longer recognized the person she had become, especially after she started shooting fentanyl.

Christine had once been a PTA and hockey mom. She loved doing things with her kids, whether it was building forts in the living room or taking them to parades such as the 2006 Steelers' Super Bowl celebration in downtown Pittsburgh. Her addiction turned Christine into exactly the kind of person she despised prior to her car accident.

She didn't work and didn't cook or help around the house. She couldn't be trusted to do much of anything with her four kids, including drive. Ironically, her days as a smoker may have saved her life. She only seemed to overdose after she went outside for a cigarette, where a neighbor could see her and call 911.

Christine finally got clean in 2016. A supportive family and the financial means to concentrate almost exclusively on her recovery saved her. Christine said most addicts don't have both of those components in place when they try to get clean; some don't have either.

"Quitting drugs was by far the hardest thing I've ever done. Hands down," Christine said. "I don't know how someone without a support system around them does it because I know how hard it is, and I have everything."

Her good fortune is why Christine puts so much time and compassion into the Sage's Army hotline. We talked shortly after a volunteer firefighter in Westmoreland County made headlines when he wrote in the comments section of a story that first responders should just let "junkies" die since they had made the choice to stick a needle in their arm. When I asked her reaction to that, Christine said, "I might have said something like that on social media back in the day if social media was as prevalent as it is now. Here I am, ten years later, saying, 'I was wrong. I was self-righteous.' "

She said people who take hard-lines stances like she once did should be careful since they may one day be touched by addiction. She is living proof that it happens.

"We need to educate," Christine said, "and stop being afraid of the stigma."

She is so far from stigmatizing addicts that Christine now says she loves them. Her drastic change in outlook is tethered to her own experience with addiction. And something even more basic.

"They're human beings," she said.

SOCIETY'S FRINGES

"Big Country," as Dave Lettrich knows him, lives on the streets in Pittsburgh and consumes sixty to eighty bags of fentanyl a day just so he won't get sick. Lettrich showed me a picture of "Big Country" with a needle sticking out of his neck. It was the snapshot of heroin addiction before the torrent of opioids, unleashed legally and illegally, dragged heroin into the mainstream.

Lettrich next clicked on a picture of a girl trapped in that tragic intersection. A year earlier she was a student at Pitt with a scholarship to study abroad in India. She comes from an affluent family with no history of substance abuse, but she started using crystal methamphetamine and heroin and almost immediately took to the streets.

When I met with Lettrich, the girl was twenty-three and living in a tent with a forty-year-old man. He made her happy because he supplied her with drugs.

That Lettrich knows her story is telling of the kind of trust the Latrobe resident builds with the addicts who are as far gone as you can get this side of death. Such intimacy is also an example, albeit an extreme one, of the care and compassion that Dr. James Han said is too often lacking when dealing with addiction.

Lettrich gravitates toward people society shuns, seeking them out at least one a week, usually on Pittsburgh's South Side. He sits and talks with them and treats them like they are any other person. They use in his presence but that doesn't bother Lettrich.

"That, to me, is an indication of their comfort level with me," said Lettrich, who ministers to addicts through Bridge to the Mountains, his nonprofit organization. "When I gain someone's trust to the point where they're not afraid to pull out a needle in front of me, I know I've got their confidence enough to help them. That I'm in a position that nobody else is in."

Lettrich, who graduated from the Pittsburgh Theological Seminary in 2018, once envisioned going to Africa and traveling by foot to refugee camps in Sudan, Uganda, and Kenya. He spent six months putting together a plan for his Africa mission, but when it came time to write that vision for a scholarship application, he continually drew a blank. He prayed about it and spent hours telling God that he was sure He wanted him in Africa.

Shortly before the application deadline, Lettrich received a different answer during a service at Hot Metal Bridge Church in Pittsburgh. A girl whose trust he'd gained entered the church in a panic. She and a friend had used in a nearby South Side restaurant/bar, and the girl overdosed in the bathroom.

Lettrich and the friend checked different hospitals before finally finding the girl and learning that she would live. He sensed an opening. He told the girl who found him at the church that if she ever wanted to stop living that way to let him know. The next morning she told him that she was ready to try a rehabilitation program. Lettrich got her into Father's Heart. When they arrived at the Jeannette faith-based treatment facility, the girl told Lettrich she'd never been more ready to get help.

This was a girl so deep in addiction that she prostituted herself, a girl who once developed a case of cellulitis so severe from constant injections that she spent three days in the intensive care unit of a hospital.

That she had accepted help nine months after Lettrich met her confirmed that he had found his calling.

"I just know this is what I've got to do," he said.

Lettrich, who grew up in an upper-middle class household, spends three hours a week among those living like a community in tents. He chats them up as they shoot up, like it is as normal as if they are putting on suntan lotion. To Lettrich that *is* his mission: treating them like the people they are, flawed and vulnerable as the rest of us.

"They need pastoral care and have the same needs that we all have," he said. "What I focus on is not are you high or are you going to get high but how is your day? When somebody is high as a kite on opioids, you can learn a lot about them and sit and have some amazing conversations. You can find out what makes them tick and what makes them hurt and where all of this comes from. You find out that they've got lot of stuff they really need to talk about."

Lettrich sees something in them that, because of their addiction, they cannot see themselves.

That is why he stays in touch with them through text messages and phone conversations. It's also why he lets them know where they can get a hot meal or a warm bed and exchange dirty needles for clean ones.

His ministry offers a stark contrast to his own view of the opioid epidemic.

"It's the most evil force we could ever imagine," he said. "It robs people of their souls. It tricks them into believing that it's what they need to live. It's beyond anything we can comprehend for those of us who have never experienced it. It makes wonderful, loving, caring people do horrible things."

Lettrich experienced that long before he hit the streets of Pittsburgh.

Years earlier, he and his then-wife got to know a young girl through her uncle. She babysat their two daughters and even went on vacation with them. Lettrich, who owned a construction company at the time, hired her when she was twenty to work part-time in the office. He soon discovered that she was stealing from him and writing bad checks.

"It turned out she was addicted to Oxycontin," he said. "That was my first introduction to opioids, and that was back in 2007. I had no idea that Oxycontin was an opiate or even the similarities between heroin and Oxy."

He got quite an education.

He and his wife moved the girl in with them and got her on a treatment regimen that included Suboxone and intensive therapy. She still struggled with addiction and bounced in and out of rehab. She spent her twenty-first birthday in jail after robbing an Eat'n Park restaurant at gunpoint.

"It was pretty much a train wreck of a time period where I learned pretty much everything you can about what it's like to live with someone with an addiction and what opioids do to people," Lettrich said. "I saw a very bright, sweet, loving girl just do horrific things for opioids."

Lettrich said she found God while incarcerated and had been clean in the one-and-a-half years since getting released from prison. He is guardedly optimistic about her future in part because of the obstacles many recovering addicts face after getting clean. The point is that she has a chance, something that applies to all addicts.

Hope is why Lettrich seeks out addicts that society has cast aside. He shakes his head in disgust when he hears talk about placing limits on Narcan for people who chronically overdose.

"You can't help anybody if they're dead," Lettrich said. "Where would the (death rate) be without the three-and-a-half million doses of Narcan that were distributed in 2017? I hate hearing that argument that it's an enabler. It doesn't enable shit. If somebody is as sick as a dog and they literally feel like they are going to die if they don't get this drug, they're going to use it, whether Narcan is there or not."

A MOTHER'S VOW

The honest obituary wasn't honest enough.

Carol Lubovinsky made that clear as we sat in a booth at Leo's Grille in Mount Pleasant, not much more than a couple of football fields away from where her daughter's funeral was held.

It had been almost two months since Carol buried her only daughter—and just two days after she and her grandsons took a birthday cake to the cemetery for what would have been Amanda Hixson's twenty-seventh birthday. Carol feelings were as raw as they were wide-ranging and for good reason.

She continues to raise her grandsons without financial assistance from their respective fathers. She doesn't know if she will ever have a relationship with her granddaughter, the youngest of Amanda's three children, since that child has mostly lived with foster parents. And, like any parent who has lost a child, she struggles with what she could have done differently.

Amanda died after overdosing on heroin laced with fentanyl, and Carol insisted on transparency in her obituary. The last part of the obituary read: *"As a note of special awareness: Amanda died from cardiac arrest caused by many years of heroin abuse that started after pain pill addiction. This has to stop. It's killing our society."*

It was a powerful passage, and yet it wasn't strong enough for Carol. Someone in the family, she felt, hedged it a bit by writing that Amanda died from a heart attack. It left Carol wondering if it looked like she was trying to hide the real reason why Amanda died. Carol was still so disgusted by the stigma that prevailed Amanda's death that she wasn't speaking with her mother. The reason: her mother told people that Amanda died of a heart attack.

"She is in complete denial," Carol said.

Writing an honest obituary was never a question for Carol after what happened more than twenty years earlier when she lost a cousin to drugs. He died after overdosing on crack cocaine, but it was hushed up. Carol said the story was spun into fumes from a dryer as the cause of death.

"I thought that was the stupidest thing any parents could do, lie about how their kid died," she said. "If you cover it up, nothing gets solved, and I won't bury my grandsons the same way (as Amanda)."

Carol and her husband have raised Bobby and Eban since 2013 after Carol was awarded full custody of Amanda's sons. She is fiercely protective of them because she doesn't want them to repeat the mistakes their mother made and because they have already experienced so much turmoil.

Neither boy has a relationship with his father. They only saw their mother a handful of times after Carol became their full-time caretaker. One of those visits left Bobby in tears. It happened when Amanda returned from North Carolina to visit. She brought Lizzy, her third child, with her when Lizzy was just a baby, and that created confusion. The day Amanda left, Bobby broke down crying at school.

"He wanted to know why his mom loved Lizzy more than him because she was leaving with Lizzy, but he stayed," Carol said while dabbing at tears.

Bobby and Eban each ask about their sister, and Carol is hopeful they will develop some sort of relationship with her. Lizzy's current foster parents are planning to adopt her, and Carol maintains contact with them.

She worries about her grandsons because they have dealt with loss and feelings of abandonment at such a young age. The saddest part of Carol's story is that Amanda appeared to turn a corner before the relapse that killed her.

Carol was always skeptical about Amanda's recovery attempts because of her unreliable behavior, failed rehab stints, and the stealing.

Despite her struggles, Amanda started prying herself from the grip of addiction in January 2018. She got clean and faithfully attended Narcotics Anonymous meetings. She did so well in recovery that she completed the requirements mandated by Washington County Children & Youth Services to get Lizzy back from foster care. She also agreed to start paying for supervised visits with Bobby and Eban. The hope was that one day they, too, would be reunited with their mother. What gave Carol hope during this time was a Facebook post Amanda wrote less than a month before she died.

"She took accountability," Carol said, "for the first and only time."

Three months after that apparent breakthrough, Carol was still trying to figure out what happened. Amanda once had such an idealistic streak that Carol told her to concentrate on herself because she couldn't save the world.

A contentious divorce with Carol's first husband (Amanda's father) may have led Amanda to start taking prescription pain pills with friends from Yough High School. Carol said that most of Amanda's friends from that time are addicts who also moved from pills to heroin.

Shortly before she overdosed, Amanda had surgery to repair a heart valve that was damaged by years of drug abuse. Carol wonders if she was given narcotics at the hospital or if she simply relapsed from the stress of everyday life. All she knows is that Amanda's phone showed that she called two different drug dealers right before the overdose that killed her.

Amanda's death has left more questions than answers, which makes Carol like most parents who have lost a child to an overdose. This includes grappling with guilt.

"To some extent, I almost feel like I put Amanda in the ground. I kicked her to the curb because I wouldn't enable her," Carol said. "I wouldn't make it easier for her to get high."

She did exactly what experts say to do when navigating the fine line between helping and enabling an addict. That included giving Amanda an opening to get her sons back, provided she rebuild the trust she shattered.

"I wanted her to step up and take accountability, and she finally did," Carol said softly.

Carol repeated a vow she made earlier in the interview when she said her grandsons would bury her, not the other way around. At the end of our talk I saw something I felt like I needed almost as much as Carol: the smile that spread across her face.

It happened as she talked about the new addition to the family. Harley Hixson, her new granddaughter, had been born earlier that week. She was coming home that day with Carol's son and daughter-in-law.

Carol couldn't wait to go see her.

ALTERNATE UNIVERSE 3

STRANGLEHOLD OF ADDICTION

To understand addiction and its insidious talons, consider Diana Shea's story *after* the Kittanning resident snorted too much crystal methamphetamine, and her "friends" told her if she died they would strap weights to her and toss her into a river.

After regaining coherency, she left and went to her parents' house. She hadn't slept for a week, and on the seventh day started hallucinating. She smoked marijuana in her bedroom to try to calm down. She closed her eyes and saw a lit doorway with a man wearing a top hat standing in it. He entered the room, as if he had come for her soul, and it scared her. She asked God to take her if He wanted her.

When she woke up, she felt foggy and had no idea how long she'd been asleep or if she were even alive. Diana walked out to the kitchen and asked her mother if she could see her because she felt invisible. "Mom? Can you see me?" she screamed.

She asked her mother to hit her. Her mother cracked her across the face. That was how Diana knew she was still alive. In a disgusted tone, her mother told her that she'd slept for seventeen hours.

"That's the last time I did meth," Diana said.

It was, however, far from the end of the drug-fueled descent that cost Diana her daughter, dignity, and dad. Ultimately, she only got two of those three back. Clean since her "surrender date" of July 15, 2015, Diana's story runs along parallel tracks of heartbreak and hope.

Her story would resonate with many addicts. Growing up, she felt awkward and shy and had trouble making friends. The need to fit in— and the desire to push back on a strict upbringing—led her to alcohol and drugs. By fifteen, she was a "full-blown alcoholic" and going down a dangerous path.

Diana started smoking crack in her twenties, which led to arrests for receiving stolen property and possession of drug paraphernalia. Only pregnancy and jail kept her clean but not for long. One day, she stumbled upon stacks of $100 bills that her father had stashed away for his retirement.

She peeled off a couple of bills to buy crack, telling herself it would end there. She blew through $15,000 in a month. She tried selling crack to replace the money but smoked the profits. She bought $700 in scratch-off lottery tickets, hoping for a big win. That Hail Mary didn't work either.

Her father, a dedicated steel mill worker, eventually found out about the stolen money. On Aug. 3, 2013, he told his only daughter to leave and never come back.

Even after her parents gained custody of her daughter, Shyanna, Diana continued to meander through a self-induced haze. She kept what few possessions she had in a garbage bag and moved from place to place. She spent more time in prison and a psychiatric ward. With nowhere else to go, she ended up in a house full of heroin addicts. She started snorting heroin and eventually allowed fellow addicts to shoot her up with it.

One injection went awry, leaving Diana with massive swelling in her left arm. The abscess that formed also caused excruciating pain. When she couldn't take it anymore, Diana removed the abscess with a steak knife and left a hole deep enough to expose the veins in her left wrist.

Not long after, she failed a drug test after going before a judge on an earlier drug charge and returned to prison. That probably saved her life. Diana got sick in jail and soon spent most of her time in the fetal position.

"It got to the point where my urine looked like black coffee," she said.

One day, the other prisoners on her cell block called for guards because Diana looked yellow. She was taken to the hospital and was diagnosed with Hepatitis C as well as liver failure from a blood infection.

"I spent four days chained and shackled to a bed with two armed guards on my sides," she said. "I thought that was it. I would cry and pray, 'God, not like this. Not now. I have a daughter.'"

She survived and resolved to get her life together but had another near-death experience from the blood infection. While on house arrest, Diana experienced pain in her right ear and struggled with her balance.

An MRI led to emergency surgery to remove an abscess between her skull and brain. Doctors later told Diana that she wouldn't have lived another week without the surgery.

"You would think my drug spree would be over there, right?" she said.

Instead, Diana's recovery collapsed when she didn't have the money to pay for supervised visits with her daughter. She turned to cocaine and heroin to numb the pain. Her turning point came after she smoked K2, a synthetic form of marijuana. She closed her eyes and dreamed that her daughter and family were laughing and having a good time without her.

"It was like a flash forward that let me see what I'd miss if I continued on my current path," Diana said. "I saw a fetus, and then it went black. When I woke up, I was in this house in the fetal position, and it was cold."

After she woke up, she started writing what she didn't like about herself and all of the stuff she wanted to do. Since that day, Diana has been clean.

"I was in hell, and I didn't think I could ever get out," she said. "Addiction took my soul, but I had one purpose in life, and that was my little girl. She was my rock."

Diana started going to 12-step meetings and Bible study and did volunteer work. She completed court-ordered community service and got involved with Residents Against Illegal Drugs (R.A.I.D.) to provide the Armstrong County-based, nonprofit organization with a recovering addict's perspective.

She also started telling her story for Drugs Kill Dreams, an Armstrong County initiative that has led her back to jail, this time for something good. She regained full custody of her daughter at the end of the 2017 school year, and the two are inseparable.

"She tells me she is proud of me," Diana said, "and that makes me feel good."

As if on cue, Shyanna, wandered in from another room and wrapped her arms around Diana's neck.

"I'm lucky I have the air I breathe," Diana continued. "I'm spreading awareness, so people don't have to live how I did and to make sure (Shyanna) doesn't do what I did. That's my purpose in life for her."

Diana Shea with her daughter, Shyanna. Photo courtesy of Diana Shea.

Almost losing her daughter isn't her only reminder of the price of addiction. Diana lost most of the hearing in her right ear and has a small scar on her left wrist. Both are from the botched heroin injection that almost killed her twice.

The more complicated pain to process is emotional. She hadn't talked to her parents for three years when she found out her mother was in the hospital. Diana told her pastor she wanted to see her mother. The following day the pastor got a call from her mother, saying she wanted to see Diana. The next day Diana visited her mom. She died less than a month later at the age of seventy-one.

"Had I known it would be the first and last time I saw her . . ." she said, as her voice choked with emotion. "She finally saw me clean and doing well. She felt comfortable I was going to be okay."

Diana saw her dad for the first time since he threw her out of the house at the funeral home. They hugged and cried, but he still refused to have anything to do with her. Diana sent him pictures and Shyanna's report cards to show him how well each were doing.

On Christmas, 2017, she put a gold coin that marked two years of clean time on her mother's grave. Diana included a note that read, "I wish we could have had more time to make memories." Two weeks later, her father was visiting the grave when he fell and suffered a compound fracture and internal bleeding. He was life-flighted to Allegheny General Hospital after flat-lining in the ambulance. His kidneys failed in the hospital, and he died on Jan. 14, 2018.

Diana knows that her father asked about her while she was in recovery, but they never had the chance to make peace.

"He took it to the grave with him," she said. "I just try to remember that I am making amends by taking care of my daughter, working my recovery, and taking responsibility."

She is never far from reminders of why she is fighting to stay clean. It could be smelling Shyanna's hair and seeing her smile. Or watching the news and seeing that the man who first injected her with heroin had been shot and killed.

"If I go back, I lose everything," Diana said. "I don't have another recovery in me. I've made so many changes in my life, and I'm proud of who I am."

* * *

The square formed by long plastic tables morphed into a circle.

Many of the people who moved shoulder to shoulder with their arms draped over one another were strangers. Yet they knew each other like few ever could. Their unspoken bond was forged through their common bond of white-knuckle struggle with addiction. Holding on to each other at the end of a 12-step meeting served as a poignant metaphor for how precarious clean living is for an addict. A moment of silence was held for anyone in the circle who was suffering, for the person who was going to use for the first time without realizing the consequences, and for the addict who was going to pay the ultimate price for using.

The group leader then led an abbreviated form of the prayer that is one of the bedrocks for recovery. *"God grant me the serenity to accept the things I cannot change; the courage to change the things I can; and the wisdom to know the difference."*

An hour earlier, I tried to be as unobtrusive as possible while slipping into a seat and treating the meeting with the sanctity of a church service. It didn't take long to notice something that reflects one of the sad truths about addiction: it can grab anybody.

Sitting diagonally from me was a young man with thick black hair and glasses. He wore a hooded Pitt sweatshirt and looked young enough to have come from class that day. A few seats from him sat a thin, older man in a drab green pullover. A walking cane hung on the table next to him.

The meeting started with a series of readings that reinforced self-awareness, accountability, and surrendering to a higher power. Next, key chains were awarded to those who had achieved a sobriety milestone. It got real following the "clean time" celebration when the group leader posed the question if anyone thought about using that day.

A young man with a broad chest, close-cropped brown hair, and a pencil-thin beard admitted he almost used earlier that day but was fortunate to work with friends who are also in recovery.

Another young man shared that he recently turned down an invitation to attend a formal at a nearby university to steer clear of the drinking that would take place. He declined the invite, a small but significant step in his ongoing recovery. He added that the loss of his brother to an overdose gave him motivation to stay clean.

The man with the cane told a harrowing story of how he almost tried heroin for the first time. An opiate user, he was in his drug dealer's truck and with one of his shirt sleeves pulled up when his Narcotics Anonymous sponsor called him. That stopped him, but he said he came close to trying heroin because it would have only cost $10.

"The first one's cheap," someone said.

A young girl stood up near the end of the meeting and said she was clinging to sobriety due to family drama. She said events, including the approaching two-year anniversary of her mother's death, were pushing her toward using and that she was only holding on because of a higher power.

"It's been really tough the last couple of weeks, and it is absolutely by the grace of my mother that I have not gotten high," she said in a shaky voice. "I don't want to end up like her. I don't want my dad to bury his daughter next to her mother."

Later, as I reviewed my notes and processed my observations, something jumped out. During the meeting, a man talked about his struggles, even with many years of sobriety under his belt. "I remember saying three years ago, 'Damn, this is the worst year I've ever had in recovery.' And then last year came. I remember saying, 'This is the worst year I've ever had clean.' And then this year came," he said. "Somewhere along the line, I'm having a worse year than the other two years, and I'm having a better year than both of them.'"

I read it over and over, trying to make sense of what he said. Then I remembered the reaction as he spoke, how others in the group nodded in agreement.

It made perfect sense to everyone else in that room.

COMMON GROUND

At first blush, Tim Phillips and Tony Marcocci make an odd pairing. One is a former addict, the other a detective who has spent three decades trying to stamp out drugs. Yet there is an easy back and forth between the two, an undeniable yin and yang that had me looking around for a tip jar when I met them.

"We'll take our show on the road anywhere," Tony said.

He is not talking about a stand-up act. Tim and Tony are part of the Westmoreland County Drug Overdose Task Force, which puts them together a lot while spreading awareness of the opioid epidemic, working with people in recovery, and trying to find solutions.

Just trying to keep up with the epidemic is a challenge. When I asked Tony if it is ever overwhelming, he said, "Only daily."

The irony is that Tony saw this coming. In 2002, he testified before US Congress about several alarming developments in heroin use. Crack cocaine users, he had warned, were turning to heroin (something he never thought would happen because the drugs have opposite effects on users). At the same time, Colombian heroin flooded America, and its purity levels were almost ten times higher than heroin already in the country. This was significant because people who may have eschewed heroin because they didn't want to inject themselves could now snort it and still get the same high. Ironically, many of those who believed snorting heroin wasn't as addictive eventually started injecting heroin as their tolerance increased.

The pool of potential users broadened even more as prescription medication became more prevalent due to a significant shift in modern medicine's approach to treating pain and aggressive marketing by pharmaceutical companies.

"It was the perfect storm," Tony said.

And it got worse with fentanyl and carfentanil passing heroin, not just in potency, but also in availability.

"There is no heroin on our streets. It's all fentanyl," Tony said. "Drug dealers said, 'Why are we even pissing around with heroin when fentanyl is cheaper to buy and is fifty times stronger? If I have a gram of fentanyl I can put fifty grams of (mixing) agent on top of that. So now I have fifty grams and have exponentially increased my profit.' That's why we're seeing the fentanyl."

Fentanyl is fifty to eighty times stronger than heroin. Carfentanil, an elephant tranquilizer, makes fentanyl seem like aspirin and can be bought through a web-based black market from countries, such as China and Mexico.

Tony said the danger of those heroin relatives, which are called analogues because of the similarities, is that users may think they are buying heroin when they are getting fentanyl or carfentanil with a mixing agent. That duplicitous way in which dealers increase their profit margins can turn deadly due to the sheer potency of the synthetic opioids.

Tony may have the resume of hard-boiled detective, but talk to him long enough and his approach to the opioid epidemic seemingly belies his law enforcement background.

He attacks stigma ("I hear the word *junkie,* and I want to crawl over a desk at someone") and says more inpatient treatment options, longer stays in them, and recovery programs tailored to individuals are needed. The treatment Tony sees now is too often as effective as treating a gunshot wound with a bandage.

Dr. Eric Kocian, Bishop Edward Malesic, Tim Phillips, and Tony Marcocci. Photo courtesy of the Westmoreland County Drug Overdose Task Force.

Working with Tim, who has been in recovery for almost thirty years, has no doubt influenced his views on addicts and treating addiction. The two agree on many things, including the belief that parents are too permissive. Maybe they rationalize their kids drinking and using marijuana because that is something they did in their youth, and neither is considered a hard drug.

"We tend to minimize the use of alcohol and marijuana today more than ever," Tim said. "Parents need to hold their kids accountable and be their parents. They have enough freaking friends."

Tim's views on drinking and marijuana reflect his own path to sobriety. He went to an in-patient facility in Pittsburgh in the late 1980s when he wanted to stop using hard drugs, never thinking it meant giving up drinking and smoking marijuana.

"Believe it or not," he said, "I didn't think that was too much of a problem."

He learned about addiction while in treatment and later attended Narcotics Anonymous meetings. The Greensburg resident has helped grow that organization in Westmoreland County. Tim, a certified forensics counselor and executive director of the county drug task force, said one of the challenges in combatting the opioid epidemic is getting people to look beyond the drugs. To Tim, the drugs are a symptom of a bigger problem.

"It's not just about the opiates," he said. "We're so focused on the opioids and the pain meds . . . Not that they aren't a problem. But if you took all of those away, there would still be something else. We have to look more globally at the disease of addiction."

*   *   *

The conversation took an unexpected turn after Tony left. The pivot happened when Tim referenced an earlier assertion made by Tony that, despite growing acceptance of it, marijuana is stronger and much more addictive than ever.

"When Marcocci was describing the good marijuana that's out there today, I'm thinking, 'Get me some of that because I would just like to try it to see how kick ass it would be,'" Tim said.

At first I thought he was kidding. When I asked if he really thought that, he nodded. "Normal people probably don't think like that," he said, "but that's how my thinking goes."

Tim has almost thirty years of sobriety but doesn't take it for granted. He regularly attends Narcotics Anonymous meetings and sponsors others in recovery. The latter is his way of giving back, and the former represents the work he still puts into his sobriety.

"I'm still vigilant on a daily basis because of the craziness that goes on in my head sometimes," he said. "Like that stupid marijuana example."

That example shows how maintaining a healthy respect for addiction is one of the keys to staying clean.

Like Tim, Dr. VonZell Wade is in long-term recovery and a leader in Westmoreland County's battle against the opioid epidemic. He and his wife, Laurie, run Lost Dreams Awakening, a counseling and support center in New Kensington. VonZell also works as a psychologist at Spirit Life, an inpatient drug and alcohol treatment center outside of Indiana. Clean for more than twenty-five years, he still sets strict parameters for himself.

Once a girl he was counseling called and told him she relapsed. VonZell went to her apartment to pick her up. He sent a text message when he arrived, and she asked if he was coming in. His reply:

absolutely not. That is his first rule when he hears from addicts in need. And like any distress call he receives, he took someone with him just to be safe.

VonZell employs similar boundaries outside of work. If he orders chicken wings to go from a bar, "I'm timing that order. If they say half an hour, I'm going to give them thirty-five (minutes), and when I arrive, they're going to hand me the wings and I'm going to hand them the money and leave."

Even after all of these years, VonZell doesn't dare poke the addiction beast.

"I firmly believe that I could have a drink and be alright for some time," he said. "I believe I could smoke a joint and be alright for some time. But I know what it's going to lead back to. Just because you can do it doesn't mean you should do it. Just because I can go into a bar right now and just drink Pepsi doesn't mean I should do it."

Ashley Rudnik, who celebrated her fifth year of sobriety in August 2018 has the same mindset. That explains why Ashley took extra precautions for her brother's marriage in the Dominican Republic's Punta Cana. Their resort rooms had refrigerators stocked with alcohol; pool bars were everywhere. Ashley, whose heroin addiction almost cost her a career in nursing and her life, took a fellow friend in recovery with her, so they could watch each other. Even then, temptation almost overwhelmed her.

"That was the hardest thing that I've been through in my addiction," she said.

Ashley steers clear of bars and situations where drinking occurs and faithfully attends 12-step meetings because of the foundation they provide in her recovery.

"The people in those meetings get me," she said. "If I surround myself with people who aren't addicts, I'm going to trick myself into thinking I'm not one, either. I need to remember where I came from, or I'll go right back."

The work required to maintain sobriety shows how tenuous the line is between clean living and full-blown addiction, especially with opiates.

What gave me true insight into the addict's mind also explains why overdose deaths are a national crisis. Addicts hear about an overdose death, and they gravitate toward the lethal dope, not get as far away from it as possible. I heard this from everyone I interviewed who has been in opiate addiction. Nothing surprised me more during my reporting.

"It's crazy because why would you ever run toward something that is killing people?" said Austin Hixson, a former heroin addict who has been clean for more than seven years. "It's the perfect example of how the addict's logic goes out the window. It's like a bizarro world."

The reality of that world put law enforcement officials in a damned-if-you-do-damned-if-you-don't dilemma in 2014. A potent mix of heroin and fentanyl circulated in the Allegheny-Kiski region and came in stamp bags labeled "Theraflu."

It caused a rash of overdoses. When Tony Marcocci talked to Westmoreland County District Attorney John Peck, he laid out a grim scenario. They could issue a warning through the media about the potency of drugs in the "Theraflu" stamp bags and risk addicts seeking the label. Or they could stay quiet and risk those not knowing how lethal that mix of heroin and fentanyl was when they took it. Peck ultimately went with the second option, but it seems crazy there was even a choice to be made.

That is the warped world of addiction as Ashley Rudnik knows well. One time she overdosed on heroin and had to be revived by friends. Her response after she regained consciousness: give me another bag.

"And the next day I went back. The stronger the better," she said. "My thinking was insane."

VonZell sees that frequently in his work with addicts.

"I understand the chase after you heard somebody OD'd and died. Now you've got to find that dealer," he said. "That's how we think. The average person looks at you like, 'Why would you want to go get it? It just killed someone.' The addicted mind says, 'That's some good shit.' "

VonZell calls it the "Superman syndrome" and says addicts think a lethal overdose won't happen to them.

Until it does.

TO MY ADDICTION

I met Pat Williams at Dean's Diner in Blairsville and struggled to reconcile the slightly built, soft-spoken man with a passage I had read in the book he authored about his son's addiction. In *Returning to the Light,* Pat wrote about the time Luke emptied a huge jar of spare change the family had saved for years to pay for a vacation.

When Pat discovered that Luke stole the money to buy drugs, he asked to talk to him in the backyard. A devout Catholic, Pat put his only son in a headlock and punched him in the face. Nothing more epitomizes the strain that addiction puts on families, particularly parents. Similarly, nothing illustrates the pull of heroin more than Luke's story.

He grew up the youngest of seven kids in a tight-knit family in Indiana, Pennsylvania. Luke embraced religion at an early age and had an active and happy childhood. Luke started using drugs in eighth grade, not long after the death of his grandfather, which hit him particularly hard. It eventually led to a heroin problem so severe that Pat and his wife bought a gravesite for Luke because they were sure it was going to kill him.

In his book, Pat writes about the time Luke was at a party and was handed a needle that he knew was infected with Hepatitis C. He plunged it into his arm anyway. Pat also included several of Luke's blog posts in the book, including one Luke wrote while at Gateway Rehabilitation Center in Monroeville:

To my addiction,

After almost nine long years, it is time to say goodbye. Before I can leave you to rest, there are some words I must say to you. @#$% you, addiction. You have brought me nothing but pain. Sure, you made it seem fun in the beginning. But every time I was vulnerable, you stuck out your ugly head. @#$%, you for letting me hurt the ones I love. I wish for you to not affect me negatively again in any way. Today I kill you. You no longer have a hold over me. You can try to sneak back up on me, but I am now strong to your evil ways. You told me I didn't deserve love; you told me I wasn't @#$%, Well, @#$%^& you, you aren't @#$%, I will not succumb to your tricks. You offered me happiness and delivered pain. You deceived me into thinking I couldn't be myself without you. But now I see that you wanted me to stay by myself, so I could live in solitude with you. I lost my fiancé to you. So I say, dead you will remain. Why did I choose you over Rachael, my family, and my integrity? You are nothing but false hope and a quick fix to a bigger problem. With you I felt nothing. You broke me and made me numb. Now I feel again, and for the greatest part, I feel hatred for you. Yes, I created you, but that means I can also destroy you. You will not control me again! I will never believe your lies. I will always remember the pain that you have to offer. My friends, family, and acquaintances never saw you. You hid well within me. Now, your ugly @#$ comes out of me, and everyone can see the true me again. I know you are scared as @#$%^&*# of Gateway, for they have the tools to end you. That is why I finally tell you that you are not my friend. You are not my hope. You are not my happiness. You are not my emotions, and foremost, you are not me. So goodbye, addiction. I hope you rot in the worst pit of hell.

"You read that, and you think he'll never use again because the drug had promised so many things," Pat said. "But everything it promised, it took away. It promised he would be likeable and funny, the life of the party. It ends up being isolating, and you end up hating yourself. Yet, they're powerless to overcome it."

Indeed, Luke's raw anger toward addiction could not stop it from controlling him. It cost him a good job when he was fired from a hospital for stealing drugs. It cost him a fiancée. It cost him friends. One time, a friend told Luke and others at a party to make a beer run. He used pain patches and passed out while they were gone. He was dead by the time they returned. Meanwhile, Luke's cycle of relapsing after periods of sobriety played out so often that Pat once pleaded with Jesus's mother Mary to parent Luke because he felt powerless to help him.

Luke's family finally convinced him to try a faith-based rehabilitation center steeped in Catholicism. Just getting him there proved to be an ordeal since Luke had to get clean before entering a Cenacolo facility in Florida.

He and Pat slept handcuffed together for two weeks, so Luke wouldn't sneak out of the house. The night before they were scheduled to leave for Florida, Luke told his father that he didn't have his driver's license. He had left it with his car at a drug dealer's house because he owed the dealer money.

"I gathered up all the strength that I had and went to the drug dealer's house and rang the doorbell, not knowing what to expect," Pat said. "I knew the guy had a gun. But he gave me the ID and keys and I left. It was a very tense time."

They made it to Florida, but Pat later found out that Luke had no intention of staying at Cenacolo. He planned to sneak out at the first opportunity, but a string of rainy days thwarted the plan of ditching rehab for the Florida beaches. Luke attended a church service two weeks into his stay, and something clicked.

It was like Pat's prayer to Mary had been answered, and Luke reconnected with the church. He served a three-year commitment and then helped start a Cenacolo facility in Alabama. He spent several more years as a missionary in Argentina and Italy.

Upon returning home to Indiana, Luke became a certified recovery specialist and started working at Spirit Life, a nearby rehabilitation facility. Luke grew so passionate about his work that he eventually decided to go to nursing school. He still wanted to work in recovery but pursued a route that offered some detachment for the sake of his own sobriety. Luke had always been a sensitive person. Losing someone with whom he was working to an overdose became too emotional for him.

Such self-awareness appeared to be another marker of how far Luke had come. He still wanted to help others in addiction yet protect his own sobriety.

"I can tell you I witnessed a miracle with our son," Pat said. "If there's ever a person you would say is beyond hope, it was my son ten years ago."

He pulled his life together in other ways, too. He reconnected with a girl he had known since second grade, and they eventually got engaged. She was also in recovery, and her daughter, who lost her father to an overdose, adored Luke.

His future abounded with possibilities. Then a trampoline accident changed everything.

A FINE LINE

Kim Klingensmith took a stand. Three weeks later, she still had mixed feelings about it, and her ambivalence captured the quandary many parents face when dealing with addicted children. The Vandergrift resident reached a breaking point after one of her sons stole her friend's debit card. Kim called the police and reported the theft.

"It was the hardest thing I ever did," she said.

A mother's most primal instinct is to protect her child. But addiction tests that, especially for Kim, who has two sons in addiction.

She said both sons have stolen so often from her and her husband that their bedroom doubles as a storage facility. Everything important is kept there, and the door is constantly locked.

"You're a prisoner in your own house," said Kim, who wears the bedroom key around her neck. "When you have company, you have to say, 'Can I please put your purse in my bedroom?'"

Despite this constant stress and strain it has put on her marriage, Kim admitted that she didn't know how long the hard stance she recently took by calling the police would last.

"I stand and then I cave," she said. "Maybe I need to be angrier."

She is one of countless people who grapple with how to deal with an addicted loved one because of this counterintuitive reality: the more you help them, the more you often hurt them.

Imagine this scenario as a parent with a young adult son: he lives at home and shows no inclination to holding down a job or getting an education. You pay his cell phone bill and don't charge him for rent, food, or utilities. You cook for him and clean his room. You even do his laundry. Do this long enough and you may end up with a basement-blogging son who freeloads off you for the rest of his life.

Add drug abuse to this scenario, and you may end up killing your son because he has no incentive to change his life.

"We have many examples of parents loving their kids to death," Tim Phillips said. "They mean well. They don't know what else to do but keep giving and giving and giving."

And addicts will keep taking and taking and taking—and are particularly keen about exploiting any situation. Katrin Schall used her father's guilt to prolong her drug run. He was an abusive father and husband, driven to such behavior by the drinking that eventually killed him when he was sixty-four.

Kat and her father reconnected later in his life. In a misguided way, he tried to make up for lost time by atoning for what he'd done. He became what Kat called her "super enabler." He bailed her out of jail any time, no questions or stipulations attached. He even allowed her to sell his pain medication to support her sixty-bag a day heroin habit.

She said it is no coincidence that she finally got on a path to long-term recovery after her father could no longer enable her.

"If my father were alive, I don't know if I'd be clean," said Kat, who has been in recovery since 2011 and is a certified recovery specialist. "He'd do anything that he could to make up for all of the shit that he did, and I totally took advantage of it. Sometimes God does for us what we can't do for ourselves."

Beth Bitler is an authority on the nuances that separate enabling from supporting. She became well versed in the differences through personal experience and her job as program director at the Pennsylvania Family Support Alliance. The organization is among many taxed by the opioid epidemic. It makes relapse prevention a priority in combatting child abuse.

Bitler spent years in a relationship with an alcoholic and never understood why he couldn't stop drinking even if she paid all of the bills. She thought she was eliminating the stress that drove him to drink. But she enabled him to keep drinking instead of confronting the root causes of his addiction. And the result was predictable. He shuttled in and out of treatment facilities, and the relationship eventually failed.

"I went through that whole circle of doing whatever I could to try to make him stop," Bitler told me when we met while she was in Westmoreland County for an opioid symposium. "You get so pulled into it that you're sicker than the person who's in addiction. Family members can't understand why there's nothing you can do or say that's going to change it."

Bitler is also director of the family program at Allenwood, a drug-and-alcohol treatment facility in central Pennsylvania, and helps family members navigate the line between helping an addict and enabling them.

"You don't want to see (addicts) suffer, but there's a point where the family members have to take care of their own lives," she said. "We encourage them to do that first because family members are usually isolated, broken, angry, and hurt by the time their loved one goes into treatment. They have to spend time on themselves and then set boundaries that don't feel like abandonment. It's hard to do."

It's also complicated because family members may feel like they are getting mixed messages when it comes to dealing with an addict. On the front end, they are told not to enable, to throw loved ones out of the house if necessary. But when an addict comes out of a treatment facility, family members who have been lied to and stolen from are told that it's important to rebuild bridges that were torched by the addict. They are also instructed to change their lifestyle—it may be something like not keeping alcohol in their house—even though they are not the ones with a problem.

It may not seem fair. It is the reality of addiction.

"If the person in recovery has a supportive family, they're much more likely to stay clean," Bitler said. "But how do you engage families who are often angry, resentful, and hurt and have been harmed in every way you can imagine and then tell them they have to support their recovering loved one?"

Bitler has helped set up family recovery groups around the state to address this question. She also advises parents to make tough decisions early, so they won't have to later struggle with questions of whether they are helping or enabling. She said the best way to do this is for parents to talk to their children about addiction, as uncomfortable as it may be for them.

"You're protecting yourself by not (talking about) it because you don't want to deal with it," Bitler said. "But you teach your child to look both ways before they cross the street because you don't want them to get hit by a car. This is the same thing."

NOW WHAT?

Nate Keisel's boyish features are such that he might have trouble buying a lottery ticket without ID. So, when he told a couple he was counseling that his fortieth birthday was less than a month away, they acted with typical surprise. They asked him how it felt to get *old*. Nate was more than happy to endure the ribbing and give them the unvarnished truth.

He told them he might feel old when he's fifty but not now, not after the days he spent in a jail cell convinced that he wouldn't live past his twenty-fifty birthday.

"I'm living on borrowed time," he said.

Nate wasn't even twenty when he and some drug buddies shot fentanyl twice after extracting the gel from a patch. Nate overdosed after the second shot and apparently came out of it just in time. One of the friends told him they were about to pitch his body into a dumpster to avoid getting into trouble.

That experience didn't even put up a speed bump in his drug use. When Nate got arrested at the age of twenty-one for stealing a credit card from the restaurant his father owned, he was relieved to get caught. That's how hard he was living.

The judge in his Erie County case gave him a suspended sentence and placed him in drug court. While in the program, Nate tried medical-assisted treatment, in-patient treatment centers, intensive outpatient therapy, and halfway houses but kept relapsing. After squandering chance after chance, the judge finally placed him in prison and wrote him off as a "hopeless case."

Religion—specifically the grace afforded to him by a pastor who also got him into a faith-based treatment center—eventually freed Nate from the bonds of addiction. Not surprisingly, he went to seminary school and is now a minister.

He and his wife moved to Jeannette in 2017 and started Mosaic Community Church. Nate is active in a host of outreach activities, including raising funds to start a business in Jeannette. The business will provide jobs to people who have trouble getting them, including those in recovery, along with life skills training.

Nate's own experience in getting second chances isn't the only inspiration for this.

Three years earlier, a fifty-year-old man approached him looking for help. The man explained that he'd been in jail for more than half his life, including for assault with a deadly weapon. He badly wanted to stop dealing drugs and running the streets. His record and the fact that he didn't drive had made it all but impossible for him to get legitimate work.

Nate helped him land a job at Kentucky Fried Chicken (KFC) in Murrysville, and he and other church members drove the man to and from work. A background check prompted a regional manager to tell the store's general manager that he had to fire the man because KFC couldn't have him working with kids. The general manager refused to fire his best worker. Nate, meanwhile, wrote a letter to the regional manager, telling him that the man was around his kids on a regular basis and that he was sincere about changing.

He kept the job, and word apparently spread about his way with cooking fried chicken. Nate said the man "ended up working so hard" that the owner met with him three months after he started work and told him sales had increased 35 percent because of his cooking. He was made a team leader despite his background.

So many things had to come together for that man to have a chance at a new life after he left his old one behind. That included the transportation that was critical to his holding a job and Nate vouching for his character and encouraging him along the way. The man could have easily slipped through the cracks.

I kept coming back to his story, and the support he received, when I heard over and over the difficulty many addicts face while pursuing long-term recovery.

*   *   *

Imagine spending thirty days at a facility where you are told when to eat, sleep, watch TV, shower, and even think. Then imagine coming out of that facility with the expectation that you will do things pretty much opposite of what was ingrained in you. You wrote right-handed? Now do it left-handed. You always tied your left shoe first and then your right one? Do it the other way around. Apply those two examples to everything else you had previously done, and that is what it is like for addicts coming out of an in-patient treatment facility.

Getting help is only part of the recovery process. And it is arguably the easy part, in a relative sense, since addicts are in a structured, supervised environment as opposed to when they are back on their own.

"Many family members think if they send their loved ones to treatment, wave the magic wand, cure them, that they're going to come home and be a different person," Tim Phillips said. "It doesn't happen like that. Recovery requires ongoing maintenance and continued attention. Without that, you won't have success."

Staying clean is only part of what addicts face coming out of in-patient treatment. Many have criminal records, eliminating them from consideration for most jobs that could turn into careers. Many aren't allowed to drive, which makes getting to work difficult, as is fulfilling recovery obligations such as out-patient rehab and 12-step meetings.

Facing such new life challenges, it is hardly surprising that so many recovering addicts relapse.

"The more barriers put in their place, the more they're going to want to give up," Katrin Schall said. "I can't tell you how many times I've worked with people, and they've said, 'It's not even worth it, Kat. Why do I even try?'"

Kat can relate. Even with five-plus years of clean time, she had difficulty renting an apartment because of the felonies on her record. A family therapist she knows introduced her to the landlord and vouched for her. Kat also offered to provide a reference for every felony charge on her record. Even then, the landlord still felt like he was taking a chance on her. Kat understood.

"I'm a five-time convicted felon," she said. "Would you want me renting your apartment?"

The question reveals the chicken-or-egg conundrum when it comes to reintegrating recovering addicts to society. Many need people to take a chance on them to have a viable chance at long-term recovery. But they often don't get the chance to show they have changed because of their past. Most addicts have burned through the trust of their closest family members. Why would a stranger who owns a business or is renting an apartment take a leap of faith?

"I get why people don't want to hire me," said Bree Swarmer, a recovering addict who lives in New Castle. "But how long does one have to pay?"

Bree's scars from years of drug abuse extend well beyond the small one on her forehead, where she injected heroin. She is extremely limited when looking for a job, even though she has never been convicted of a felony. Just getting charged with a serious drug offense as she was— it was later reduced to a misdemeanor—prohibits her from working around children. She also is not allowed to work for a doctor or even a veterinarian because of the drugs in those offices.

"Your list is so narrowed down," she said. "You're stuck with addiction counseling or minimum wage."

Recovering addicts are ideal candidates to work in recovery because of their credibility with people battling addiction. They understand exactly what addicts are going through and thus are in the best position to help them. But it is analogous to professional athletes and broadcasting. They are perfect for those post-playing positions because of their experiences, but there are only so many of those jobs. The same is true for occupations in recovery. According to Tim Phillips, there are more than 200 certified recovery specialists in Westmoreland County, but only a fraction of them are making a living in that field.

"Sometimes we just need a break," said VonZell Wade, who runs Lost Dreams Awakening in New Kensington. "If you let us in, we'll show you the rest, but for crying out loud, let us in."

VonZell frequently deals with addicts' frustration as they try to rebuild their lives. He tells them to keep their head up and stay in position. The latter is a euphemism to stay clean, so they can pass a drug test if a job opportunity presents itself. He said that message doesn't always gain traction because of other pressures they face, especially after coming from an inpatient treatment facility.

VonZell cited some examples, such as telling someone to prioritize recovery meetings when they still need to find a place to live or being told to get a job without a driver's license and barely enough money for a bus pass.

He said helping recovering addicts with basic needs is critical to their recovery.

"Stress is the number one cause of relapse," VonZell said.

ALL RISE

Judge Meagan Bilik-DeFazio thought something was wrong when she heard that inmates in the Westmoreland County Prison were saying to steer clear of drug court. But the certified recovery specialists who work with drug court assured her it was a good sign because it meant that the program had some teeth.

One of Westmoreland County's more recent if belated responses to the opioid epidemic gives participants a chance to avoid jail time while weeding out anyone who is not serious about recovery. Drug court lasts at least eighteen months and participants must complete five phases before they graduate. Requirements include passing a minimum of two drug tests a week, participating (not just joining) in a recovery program, and getting a job or working in community service. Participants must also undergo a drug-and-alcohol evaluation prior to qualifying for drug court and follow the recommendation, whether it is a lengthy stay in an inpatient rehabilitation or simply outpatient treatment.

Bilik-DeFazio, who oversees the program with Judge Christopher Feliciani, said the county drug court graduated twenty-four members in its first two years.

"On graduation day, I get teary-eyed," Westmoreland County Commissioner Gina Cerilli said. "People that have completely hit rock bottom stand up in the courtroom (after) testing drug free for eighteen months, getting their bachelor's degree, or working full-time jobs. They're regaining custody of their children and mending broken relationships with their families. It's the one thing that's working."

Josh Rimmel is proof of that. The Vandergrift resident graduated from drug court in December 2017 and has stayed active in the recovery community. Josh celebrated his thirty-seventh birthday in September 2018, about a month before the three-year anniversary of his sobriety. He tells his story to high school and college students as well as people in treatment facilities and recovery houses.

Following a string of arrests, Josh was given the opportunity to enter drug court after spending seven months in jail for overdosing when his two children were with him.

He initially bristled at the length of the program but did everything required of him, including a seventy-six-day stay at Conewago Treatment Facility near Indiana. He dutifully called in every day to see if he had to take a drug test and attended 12-step meetings nearly as often. Josh never failed a drug test. He also bought into Narcotics Anonymous meetings so much that he still attends four a week.

Drug court provided the structure he needed. It also gave him every opportunity to succeed because he felt like he was treated as a person and not just a number.

"I've been in courtrooms where you just get badgered and looked down upon by judges because they're up on the bench," he said. "But to have a one-on-one conversation with a judge (Bilik-DeFazio) who actually listens to you and gives you recommendations is so helpful. Being looked at like somebody and not just as some criminal was amazing."

Even though he has graduated, Josh said he can still reach for help to anyone involved with drug court. That kind of ongoing connection is what makes the program so worthwhile to Bilik-DeFazio and Feliciani.

"Drug court is really where you feel like you can actually make a difference and impact somebody's life," Bilik-DeFazio said. "I can't imagine not doing it. I'm here until they kick me out."

Tony Marcocci, Tim Phillips and judges Christopher Feliciani and Meagan Bilik-DeFazio. Photo courtesy of the Westmoreland County Drug Overdose Task Force.

Drug court has its limitations. It can only accommodate sixty people at a time, and even those who complete the program face a bigger challenge once they leave the structure of drug court. Josh knew a girl who graduated after him but relapsed and died from an overdose. Two others he got to know from the program also relapsed.

Just as problematic for drug court participants is navigating everyday life while in the program. Many have limited options because of lost driving privileges and criminal records.

Feliciani said one participant was reported for driving without a valid license. He said the man was one of the "hardest workers" he's ever seen but one stipulation of drug court is abiding by the law. Feliciani didn't want to do it, but he put the man in jail for forty-eight hours. To him, it raised the larger question of how to help those who are genuine about recovery, especially when it comes to driving. Imagine not having those privileges; it affects every aspect of your life.

"There has to be changes within the legislature to come up with some exceptions for these people to get (around). We can't expect them to go back to being responsible if they can't drive to work," Feliciani said. "They get out of the program, and six months go by, and they still don't have a driver's license and can't get to work. I can understand their frustration. So, they're either going to start driving illegally and try to avoid the police or revert back to their earlier lifestyle. I'm not sure what the answer is, but they need to give limited licenses to people who have demonstrated sobriety in programs like this one."

A RECOVERY MODEL

Many mornings, Gus DiRenna and Rev. Jay Geisler can be found inside Gary's Restaurant, just off the main road that runs through the Carrick section of Pittsburgh. It may be a stretch to say that they're solving the nation's problems over coffee and breakfast, but then maybe it isn't. The two are in long-term recovery, and they are invested—literally, in some cases—in helping others achieve sobriety. Just as the ripples of addiction can have wide-range devastating consequences, recovery has a butterfly effect, too. Addicts who achieve it may inspire others to do the same, and as recovery spreads, lives and communities change for the better.

Of course, getting clean and staying clean are two different things. Gus and Jay, who preaches at Brentwood's St. Peter's Episcopal Church, have worked together for almost ten years to bridge what can be a yawning gap between the two. That helps explains why, shortly after I joined them at Gary's one morning, Gus, the recovery director of Allegheny Recovery Krew, switched seats with me, so he could sit on the outside of our booth. He left several times while we chatted, after flipping open a phone that may have said as much about his relatively simple lifestyle as it did his age of fifty-eight years.

His phone may be a relic, but it is critical to Gus, who sends out works crews every morning and stays in contact with them. Providing jobs to those in recovery is only part of what Gus and Jay do through their partnership. They also own or lease a handful of recovery houses in Western Pennsylvania and use them to assist people in recovery.

The houses are large enough that every tenant has their own bedroom as well as access to a kitchen, bathrooms, and a spacious community area. The bedrooms are key to their recovery houses because residents aren't forced to live on top of one another.

Rent ranges $400 to $500 a month, possibly less if a tenant takes a smaller bedroom. Employment opportunities are provided in everything from painting and contracting to work in food services through their many contacts.

Starting wages are $10, which is significantly higher than the minimum wage in Pennsylvania. The jobs allow recovery house residents to pay rent. To further help those in recovery, Gus and Jay own two vans that transport people to work and 12-step meetings. They also try to secure recovery houses that are accessible to public transportation for those who find jobs elsewhere but may not have a valid driver's license.

There are opportunities for those in recovery to learn a skill that will sustain them after they are on their own. It happened with one of their recent success stories.

Gus took a man in recovery on a job with him. On his first day, the trainee stood in a bathroom with a piece of tile in his hand and no idea what to do. He learned how to tile on the job and got so good at it that Gus finally told him to go into business for himself and make more money.

"Now he's the most sought-after ceramic tile guy around," Gus said. "He also taught some of the guys that are with me now."

That story illustrates the cycle of sobriety that Gus and Jay try to perpetuate. They offer housing that provides support and privacy at a reasonable cost. They provide job opportunities with livable wages and job-training. Those who learn a trade help teach others in recovery. Ideally, it keeps paying forward.

Their message is clear: there is a recovery model that works and sustains itself.

"It's win for the addicts, a win for the landlord, a win for the community," Jay said.

It is in the case of Teresa Takach. Clean since February 2017, Teresa was living out of her car before finding respite in the Beechview recovery home that Jay owns. The 2009 Brentwood High School graduate earned enough money from the jobs lined up for her to pay her rent. She learned a host of new skills on those jobs and can now operate a circular saw. When Teresa wanted bookshelves for her bedroom, she cut the wood and installed them herself, something she wouldn't have dreamed of doing previously.

"I've been taught everything here," she said.

Gus is the perfect person to lead an endeavor that does everything it can to help addicts achieve long-term recovery. He'd learned job and life skills before a heroin addiction cost him his family and nearly his life. He has been clean since 2010 and knows as well as anyone how tough it is maintaining sobriety, especially for those ensnared by addiction before they are even adults.

"Getting clean is one thing, but how do you navigate life after that?" he said. "If we don't help these kids get on their feet, they'll never do anything. We get them moving forward, and before long, they're pulling someone else to their feet. We've come up with a solution that really works."

SAUDADE
AND
CARMEN
CAPOZZI

SAGE'S ARMY

His aunt knelt over him and screamed to God. It didn't matter to the man tucked in the fetal position, rocking back and forth. Two days after losing his twenty-year-old son to a heroin overdose, Carmen Capozzi wanted to die.

Sage, his only son, had battled addiction for years. Carmen traced it to the medication Sage started taking for attention deficit hyperactivity disorder (ADHD). Sage moved from what Carmen calls "legalized speed" to illegal drugs and got hooked on heroin. He had been clean for ninety days when he relapsed after losing his paternal grandmother.

He overdosed in an Irwin motel room. By the time his girlfriend realized something was terribly wrong, it was too late. Carmen said goodbye to Sage in Westmoreland Hospital, a week after burying his mother, and holed up in his old bedroom at his father's house. Friends and family members streamed in and out of the house, crying with Carmen when they stopped in his room. Bill Dunn hugged him and told him he loved him. Carmen had done the same more than four years earlier after Adam Dunn was hit by a car and killed. Adam, a volunteer firefighter and accomplished dirt bike rider, was eighteen when he died, two days before Christmas. Carmen spent the holiday consoling his best friend, trying to find the right words.

He never dreamed the situation would one day be reversed.

All of it felt like an out-of-body experience. He spent most of the two days after Sage died with his knees touching his chest. When he stretched his legs, he also kicked the wall and wailed. "Why! Why! Why!" He replayed everything in his head, his mind a treadmill running in reverse. What should I have done? What could I have done? Why Sage? Why me? He thought about the last time he saw Sage, after rushing into the Greensburg hospital and hearing there was nothing more that doctors could. Even with the breathing tube jammed down Sage's throat and the instructions not to touch him because of a pending criminal investigation, it didn't seem real. Carmen rubbed Sage's brown hair and told him, "You're going to be okay. Daddy loves you. Mummy loves you. Cindy loves you. Everybody loves you. You're going to be okay."

He was still numb when he called his father—"Pap" to Sage—and told him that Sage was gone. His father unleashed a scream that Carmen will never forget. When he got to his father's house, he retreated to his old bedroom, completely broken and in his own hell. Nobody could reach him over the next two days.

Even his aunt's sharp elbows digging into his side couldn't elicit a response. Carmen never looked at her as she called out to God to help him. Later, with the room pitch black, Carmen heard a voice.

"Dad, get up. They're not bad kids. You have to help." It was Sage.

Carmen jumped up and flipped on a light. He looked around the room, positive that he could feel Sage's presence. When he emerged from his old bedroom a little after 10 p.m. and walked downstairs, his father popped out of an easy chair. He had been worried sick about Carmen and asked if he was hungry and wanted something to eat.

"Dad," Carmen said, "I've got to go home."

The next morning, he asked his longtime partner Cindy for a tablet. He had never been much of a writer, but he started scribbling furiously. That continued upon returning home after Sage's viewings and into the next day as he thought about what needed to change. Two hours before the funeral, he told Cindy, "I think I just wrote Sage's eulogy."

He read it to her, and she agreed that he had to share it. He titled it "God's Plan. My Purpose."

More than 600 people crammed into Our Lady of Grace in Greensburg for Sage's funeral. It was a typical Western Pennsylvania day in March—gray and rainy—which made what happened as Carmen delivered his son's eulogy all the stranger. He started to sweat as he memorialized Sage and had no idea why he suddenly felt like he was in a sauna.

It was pouring after the service, as a line of cars made their way to Twin Valley Memorial Park in Delmont for Sage's final farewell. En route to the burial, Sage's best friend pulled to the side of the road. He'd run out of gas at the worst time for a pallbearer. Sage and Jimbo Gerken had always formed their own comedy duo, feeding off each other's humor. The fact that Jimbo had to flag down the last car in the funeral procession couldn't have been more perfect. A joke from above. "Jimbo," Carmen later told him, "only you."

After the burial, Jimbo's mother rushed up to Carmen and excitedly asked if he had seen it. That it had stopped raining as Carmen delivered the eulogy. That a beam of sun, as unbreakable as a slab of steel, had settled on him. "Carm," she said, "Sage came to you." It could have been dismissed as a simple coincidence. But taken with the voice he heard in his old bedroom, it made Carmen wonder if there were indeed higher forces at work.

That night family and friends held a vigil at Carmen and Cindy's house. They told Sage stories and shared laughs.

One of Carmen's favorite stories sheds light on Sage's personality. It happened when Sage met Civil War battle reenactors in Bedford, Pennsylvania. Sage was only ten at the time but was fascinated by the military, and the group quickly took a liking to him. They even gave him a part in the reenactment. Sage had told the reenactors that his father played the drums, so they cast him as a drummer on the Confederate side.

He couldn't actually play the drums, so it was decided that he would hand them off to someone else right before the battle started. Not that Sage receded into the background after playing his part. The cannons started going off to signify the start of the battle, and Sage fell over in exaggerated fashion. All Carmen could do was shake his head and laugh.

He listened to more Sage stories that night and tried to keep it together. But when Carmen hugged his niece near the end of the vigil, something snapped. His legs buckled. His stomach churned. The pain of losing Sage was as overwhelming as the night he died. Carmen dropped to his knees and started bawling. His uncle Tony picked him up and carried him up to his bedroom.

It was the same uncle who had carried him out of Westmoreland Hospital after Carmen saw Sage alive for the final time.

* * *

Time seemed to crawl after Carmen buried his only child. The days blended together as Carmen looked at picture after picture of Sage. The memories that flooded his consciousness made it that much harder to accept that Sage would never walk through his front door again.

A week after Sage's death, Nick Ringling, one of Sage's friends, visited Carmen and Cindy. They watched TV and looked at messages on the Sage Capozzi Memorial Page. One said how funny Sage was and how he'd always been there for her. She wrote that kids sometimes picked on her because she was overweight. One time, Sage saw it happening on the bus and told everyone to stop. He sat with the girl every day for the rest of the school year.

The president of Westmoreland County Community College wrote that she'd worked with Sage and gotten to know him well. She too was devastated to hear of his death. Something hit Carmen as he read the testimonials, including things he never knew, on Nick's laptop computer.

"Nick," he said, "Sage's heart was good. He was always trying to help his friends. I need to create awareness. I need an army of people." Nick looked at him and said, "Cool. Sage's Army." He started tapping away on his laptop. After a couple of minutes he handed it to Carmen. He had started a Facebook page titled Sage's Army and tagged twenty of his friends to it. "Check it tomorrow," Nick said.

The next morning Carmen awoke and needed a reason to leave the house. He hadn't been to work since his mother died almost three weeks earlier, so he drove to Ligonier to check on the crew from the flooring company that he owns.

He arrived at the house of Sandy Mellon, where his crew was working. When he walked into the industrial-sized kitchen, her head snapped around like she had been slapped in the face. He explained why he was there. She told him if he needed to check on his workers then he needed to find a new crew. She wrapped him in a hug and said, "Honey, go home." *To what?* Carmen thought to himself.

He started to leave but barely made it through the front door when he encountered a man standing in front of him, crying and shaking. It was one of the groundskeepers. He'd known Sage through Carmen's business, and he commented on how nice he was. He said he had no idea that Sage battled a drug problem. Carmen's mind returned to Sage's viewings and how many parents told him that they too had a child in addiction.

"We all stayed silent," he told the man.

The two hugged, and the man told Carmen about a clearing at the top of the mountain that he might want to check out. The Mellon family patriarch had put a bench there that lent itself to thinking and introspection. Perhaps Carmen could find a little peace there. Carmen got into his truck and followed a street that winded through woods. He stopped when he saw the bench in the distance.

Tall trees, most of them straight as a cadet, lined a grassy plateau. They formed a chute that narrowed out to a spectacular view of hazy mountain ranges. Carmen felt like he could see forever, and he soon spotted a rock that looked out of place. It was embedded in the ground and much of it was covered by thick moss. It was the only rock Carmen could see, so he went to it.

He stood on it. He sat on it. He knelt on it. He cried, and he screamed to God. "Why? Why? Why? Why? Why did you do this to me? Why did you take my son? What did I do to deserve this? Why? Why? Why? Why?" His torrent of grief echoed off the trees for hours until he finally scared himself enough to wonder if God might answer him with a bolt of lightning.

Sage and Carmen Capozzi. Photo courtesy of Carmen Capozzi.

When Carmen returned home, completely drained, he turned on his laptop computer and nearly did a double take. He shouted, "Cindy!" and she came running from her office. The days since Sage passed had been hell for her, too. She loved him like a son, and her grief was compounded by her worry for Carmen. "What's the matter? What happened?" she said. Carmen showed her the Facebook page that Nick started the previous night. "Look!" he said pointing to it. Eighteen-hundred people were already signed up for the Sage's Army page. Carmen and Cindy couldn't believe it. There were messages from people all over the country, including a woman from California.

One post really resonated with Carmen. It came from Avi Israel, founder of Save the Michaels of the World outside of Buffalo, New York. Avi's son had committed suicide nine months earlier after years of battling Crohn's Disease and then an opiate addiction.

When the two connected over the phone, they talked for hours. Avi told Carmen how Michael had been prescribed into addiction because of the pain and anxiety caused by Crohn's Disease. Avi said that Michael's addiction took him and his wife, Julie, through a labyrinth of doctors, treatment centers, and insurance companies that led nowhere. He told Carmen about June 4, 2011. That day Michael took a shotgun he had hidden under his bed and shot himself in the head. Avi kicked in the door to Michael's bedroom after hearing the blast but couldn't save him. Michael was the same age as Sage when he died. Shortly after that, Avi retired from his job as an electrician and became a full-time advocate at the age of sixty-two.

Talking to Avi and reading the different messages on Sage's Army Facebook page—some offering to help, some asking for help—caused Carmen to flash back to hearing Sage: *Dad, get up. They're not bad kids. You have to help.*

Carmen got up then, not sure what to make of it. That message made sense to him now, his purpose as clear as the sky had been earlier that day.

He wasn't sure how he was going to lead or if he was even ready to lead. But Carmen knew a thing or two about making noise. Carmen played the drums in different bands going back to high school, and he passed his love of music on to Sage.

He had stayed quiet far too long. Now, he was about to bang a different kind of drum.

TRAGEDY AND PURPOSE

A charter bus filled with people wearing Sage's Army T-shirts rolled from Irwin to Washington DC on October 1, 2013, for the inaugural Fed Up rally. The movement sought to bring awareness to the opioid epidemic and pressure lawmakers to take action, including reclassifying addictive pain medication to make it more difficult to prescribe.

Carmen briefly met with Pennsylvania State Representative Tim Murphy and then took a taxi to the Food and Drug Administration building. More than 800 people had gathered there. As he searched for Sage's Army shirts in the cluster of bodies, he heard, "Carrr-men!" He looked around and saw a man running toward him. He had never seen the man before, but they knew each other well. Like Avi, David Humes reached out to Carmen shortly after Sage died, and they formed a bond over the loss of their sons.

David introduced himself, and he and Carmen hugged and cried.

"Avi is asking where you are," David said. "Let me take you to him."

They quickly found Avi, and as he and Carmen hugged, Avi whispered into his ear that he had held Michael as he took his last breath. "I knew I had to do something," he said. "Just like you, Carm."

That day David, Avi, and Carmen were among those who demonstrated in front of the FDA building. Carmen told a story about the small shovel his dad kept from his stint in the army and its powerful symbolism. Sage always loved the military and once insisted on using it to help Carmen build a retention pond. "This is Pap's shovel," Sage said firmly any time Carmen asked him if he wanted to dig with something bigger.

Carmen held up the shovel as he addressed the crowd and said, "We're going to tear down a mountain with this shovel!"

The inspiration that day provided couldn't mask the tragedy of why Avi, Carmen, and David were there. And what binds them also reflects what is happening all over the country. Too many parents are losing children to the opioid epidemic, no matter where they live.

I spoke with David Humes more than four years after he met Carmen for the first time—and a day after he went before the Delaware legislature as a full-time activist. He lives outside of Wilmington, which is large enough to serve as a state capital yet small enough to be considered a suburb of Philadelphia.

David lost his son, Greg, to a heroin overdose on May 15, 2012—a little more than two months after Sage died. Greg's experimentation with drugs and alcohol in high school escalated into cocaine use. Near the end of his senior year, he told his father and stepmother that he needed help. Greg went to a rehabilitation facility shortly after graduating but relapsed and eventually moved to heroin. His addiction landed him in prison but that seemed to be the wake-up call he needed. After getting out of prison, he stayed clean for seventeen months before running into a couple of old friends in Philadelphia.

Greg overdosed that night, and his friends drove his car to a hospital. They left the car, with Greg in the passenger seat, in the parking lot. He wasn't found for an hour. By then it was too late, and Greg died at the age of twenty-four. His friends were too scared to call the police or take Greg into the hospital. They may have been too panicked or high to call 911 anonymously or press the panic button on Greg's key fob before they left the car.

A detective later told David that had his friends not left him in the parking lot, Greg's life could have been saved. David's birthday fell on the same day that he identified Greg's body. The two had planned on celebrating David's birthday at a Phillies game that night, the perfect gift for David since he and Greg loved baseball and bonded over it.

Of seeing Greg's body on the day that was supposed to be one of celebration, David said, "That's my birthday every year now because of that."

David vowed to Greg that he would save a life in his memory and "As I like to say, then I got greedy. One wasn't enough."

Indeed, David lobbied to break down the barriers that prevented Greg from getting the emergency help he needed. A little more than a year after Greg's death, Delaware Governor Jack Markell signed the Good Samaritan Act into law. The law allows anyone to call first responders in the case of an overdose without fear of getting arrested. The following year, David attended the ceremony that marked the passage of a bill that provides Narcan to Delaware police officers.

David also helped pass the Good Samaritan Act in Pennsylvania, which took considerably longer because Pennsylvania has more layers of bureaucracy due to its size. Passing the law in Pennsylvania was significant to David since Greg died there and might have lived with such a law in place.

David started atTAcK Addiction not long after Greg died and closed his construction business at the age of sixty-one to run the nonprofit organization full time.

David's story reminded me of something Michelle Schwartzmier said when I met her a couple of months earlier. "There is Michelle, the advocate, and Michelle, the grieving mother." Keeping them compartmentalized is very difficult if not impossible because the grief is always there.

"There are times when it hits you in the face like a two by four," David said. "It comes out of nowhere and just smacks you in the face. It doesn't go away."

It could be something as routine as providing information at a doctor's office. When David saw a specialist about a shoulder problem, the doctor asked how many children he has. He said, "Two. I have one living."

David rejoiced like other Philadelphia sports fans when the Eagles beat the New England Patriots in the 2017 Super Bowl, ending a title drought dating back to 1960. But it wasn't the same without Greg there to watch the game with him. Just like the previous summer when David's other son got married, a time of great happiness also brought sadness since Greg should have been the best man in the wedding.

David has "Saudade" on the vanity plate of his car. He got it after a friend of Greg's told him about the Portuguese word and its greater meaning.

"It's an instance when you can feel both joy and sadness at the same time," David said. "A prime example is Father's Day. I have the joy of being with my son and the sadness of my son who isn't there. It's a very emotional term yet I find it comforting. It really does capture what you feel on a day-to-day basis."

In a perfect world, David would've worked with Greg in his construction business and turned it over to him when he retired. Greg had a keen eye when it came to details of the business, and David is sure he would've been successful with it.

Instead, he sold the business after Greg died, so he could advocate full-time. Whether he is lobbying for legislation or bringing awareness to the opioid epidemic, David is guided by the premise that Greg was a good kid who made a tragic mistake by trying heroin.

"Through Greg's entire life, the one word always used to describe him was sweet," David said. "This includes a neighbor meeting him and briefly talking to him for the first time. It seems a lot of young people struggling with addiction are just the opposite of what people stereotype them as. In most instances, they're really kind people that have been taken to a bad place."

That often extends to parents. Many are too embarrassed to admit that their child struggles with addiction out of fear of being judged. David sees stances toward addiction softening but thinks there's still a lot of work to be done.

"A lot of people say, 'They made the decision. Too bad.' My answer to them is in some instances, such as my son, it may have been a decision the first time. But once you've used (heroin), the addiction is almost immediate," he said. "And my follow up to that is how would you like to be judged for the rest of your life for making one bad decision when you were in your late teens or early twenties and your brain wasn't fully developed? Plus, the statistics are such that 80 percent of injection heroin users started with legally or illegally prescribed opiates. So for the vast majority, it wasn't their decision."

That is what happened to Avi Israel's son. In 2010, Michael told his parents that he was addicted to his prescribed pain and anxiety medication. But doctors were generally dismissive when Avi and his wife, Julie, raised concerns. Avi and Julie saw the problem with their own eyes when Michael went into the hospital after his intestines closed.

"Every time he got a shot of pain meds it was the look of someone getting high," Avi said. "My wife and I informed the surgeon that something was not right with Michael. You could see it on his face, and he kept asking for another pill or shot. We were told he'd be weaned off it before he left the hospital."

Michael spent two months in the hospital and, Avi said, doctors continued to load him up with painkillers. He had two surgeries during his stay and left the hospital with one hundred Hydrocodone pills, ninety Xanax pills, and two disgusted parents.

"That's how they weaned him off," Avi said.

As Michael's addiction escalated, his parents dealt with feelings of helplessness. They had learned everything about Crohn's when Michael was diagnosed with the inflammatory bowel disease. They changed their diet, so Michael wouldn't feel left out and encouraged him to pursue model building, something that gave him a feeling of control.

But they knew almost nothing about addiction and didn't get much help in trying to treat it. No one seemed to know of a treatment center where they could send Michael. When Avi found one, it turned out to be a facility that treated alcohol addiction. Michael spent three days there before he was sent home because the insurance company refused to pay for his treatment.

Avi received a text a month later from Michael: "I love you, Dad. You don't deserve a son like me."

Avi called 911 as he raced home from work. Julie found Michael in their garage with the car running. The suicide attempt landed Michael in the psych ward of the local hospital, but he was released after twelve hours. His father tried to find a treatment center for his opiate addiction but none that he contacted had an open bed. Michael shot himself on June 4, 2011.

After his death, Avi and Julie started Save the Michaels of the World to confront problems they encountered with Michael's addiction. A little more than a year after Michael killed himself, the Michael David Israel Law went into effect in New York. The eponymous law created an online database that tracks opioid prescriptions in the state, preventing people from doctor- or pharmacy-shopping to obtain prescription medication.

The nonprofit organization also advocates for laws that make it more difficult for insurance companies to deny treatment for addiction and mandates education for doctors when it comes to prescribing medicine. There were twenty-five in-patient beds for addicts in western New York when Save the Michaels of the World launched. There are now more than 200, Avi said.

"We did a lot of good, but we also realized that there is no awareness when it comes to addiction," Avi said. "Nobody wants to talk about addiction because it's taboo. We're trying to erase that and bring addiction to the forefront. If (an addict) is telling you 'I'm ready to go to treatment' you can't tell them to come back in three days. You will never see someone with diabetes or someone who suffers from cancer that has to wait in line anywhere. Addiction should be treated the same way."

Providing access to treatment is only part of the equation. Avi's nonprofit organization also focuses on helping addicts after they finish treatment. There aren't nearly enough resources devoted to this, and the general message to addicts is that they are largely on their own after treatment. Save the Michaels of the World addresses this by getting families involved in recovery. It may be something as simple as persuading family members to change their behavior to help the addict or working with the addict on a long-term recovery plan.

Grassroots organizations such as Sage's Army, atTAcK Addiction, and Save the Michaels of the World are critical to battling the opioid epidemic for several reasons. They are on the front lines of it and aren't encumbered by the bureaucracy that hinders government agencies. Just as important are the people driving these organizations. They're imbued with passion and anger, which inspires others around them and prompts communities to act.

Like David and Carmen, Avi paid a horrific price to reach the vanguard of a movement.

He and Michael were very close. They shared a love of airplanes, reading, and the New York Yankees. They went to air shows, and Sundays were reserved for Barnes & Noble, where they'd sit for hours and lose themselves in a good book. Michael couldn't get enough of reading Jack Kerouac, watching Derek Jeter, or building model airplanes that were so meticulous they included oil leaks.

The gains Avi's organization has made are tempered by his enormous personal loss. Some days are still so bad that Avi will shut off his cell phone for hours and think about Michael. That explained why I couldn't reach him on one of the days we were scheduled to talk.

When we did connect, Avi told me about a benefit he attended the previous night. It was organized by people who have been helped by Save the Michaels of the World. Parents thanked Avi for helping save their son or daughter. People in recovery thanked him and Julie for saving their lives.

It was a night of *saudade.*

"We lost our child but we're able to help other people live," Avi said. "It doesn't make what happened to Michael okay. It just puts in perspective that Michael's legacy is living on through other people."

FINDING SAGE

Sage's death led Westmoreland County native Rich Jones to make a life-changing decision. Rich counseled Sage as part of Outside In's drug-and-alcohol program, and they'd grown close. He saw Sage, who was sent to the juvenile facility after getting caught breaking into cars, blossom with the structure he received at Outside In. Sage emerged as a leader and earned the highest status in the program, one that few attain.

"You couldn't have done better in treatment then that kid did," Rich said. "What was missing was there was nothing to help guide the family when he returned home. The kid wouldn't do the (post-treatment) recovery program on his own, and the family didn't know what to do."

The gap that Rich, a recovering addict, identified from his experience with Sage led him to a career crossroads. He felt he could no longer work within the confines of clinical counseling. The opioid epidemic, as he saw it, demanded a new approach. That is why Rich flipped the counseling model and now seeks out those who need help, instead of the other way around, through Faces and Voices of Recovery (FAVOR).

He relocated to South Carolina and started FAVOR less than a year after Sage's death. The nonprofit organization relies solely on donations but is not encumbered by stipulations that would exist if it accepted government money.

"I left a cushy-ass job, and people thought I was crazy," said Rich, a native of Stahlstown. "They were like, 'You're going to be living in a van down by the river. You think people are going to donate money to do this?'"

They have, and Rich and his colleagues go to emergency rooms, schools, and homes, wherever an addict needs help. They often connect through families trying to navigate the terrifying world of addiction. They form bonds with addicts through consistent calls and visits. They deliver services instead of waiting for addicts to come to them.

Rich said that's impossible to do in clinical settings because of insurance regulations and rules of engagement. Counselors are told to establish boundaries with patients outside of work and are encouraged to walk the other way if they see a patient in public. Rich does the opposite because it enhances connections, which are critical to treating addiction.

Engagement is the foundation of FAVOR's mission since it is widely agreed by experts that 90 percent of people in addiction don't seek help.

"They won't go to a clinic; they won't go to a 12-step meeting," he said. "As a society, we have traditionally said that they have to hit bottom and want (sobriety) bad enough, and then they'll show up. What that approach has resulted in is 65,000 people dying every year from an opioid use disorder and another 88,000 dying from alcohol use disorder. We have said, 'We're going to come to you.'"

Rich is convinced this approach could have saved Sage's life. He said Sage did "great" in peer settings but had trouble connecting with 12-step programs. That may have been because people in those groups were usually older than Sage. It may also have been because he was still in his late teens, where thinking you know everything is a hallmark of that age but also gives oxygen to addiction.

"If (Sage) had a person assigned to him whose job it was to connect with him over and over for five years, it could have been different," Rich said. "What if our system had an ability to pay for a coach for five years where that coach is not allowed to come back and say he couldn't find Sage."

Losing Sage years before he died led to many sleepless nights for Carmen. He didn't know how to handle Sage's addiction by the time he realized the severity of it. He missed the signs that preceded full-blown addiction because he didn't know what to look for. When Sage was moody, he attributed it to typical teen behavior or perhaps girl problems.

Sage hid his addiction well, but when he did get caught using he was punished. Carmen grounded him and revoked his driving privileges. When that didn't work, he took away golf and his guitar, two things Sage loved. But that also put Carmen in an impossible situation. He had to punish Sage but also knew that playing his guitar and writing songs were an outlet for working through his problems. The final week of Sage's life illustrated how tough it is for a parent dealing with a child in addiction. He relapsed following the death of his grandmother. Carmen and Cindy drug-tested him after they suspected something wasn't right, and he tested positive for cocaine. Carmen gave him an ultimatum: get back in your recovery program or leave the house. Sage chose the latter. But even after he left, Carmen said they talked multiple times a day until Sage went back to heroin and fatally overdosed.

"Carmen did everything by the book," Rich said. "He practiced setting boundaries. He did what he was told to do. Ideally, there should have been somebody professionally trying to find Sage and help him. That's what a recovery coach does."

In retrospect, Carmen said the thing best thing for Sage is something that is counterintuitive to a father who wants to protect his child.

"I wish I could go back in time and tell police to bust my kid. Get him off the street," Carmen said. "But the last thing a parent wants is for a kid to go to jail because they think it's going to ruin their life."

Out of desperation, Carmen went to the police a year before Sage died. He feared for Sage's life and Carmen signed paperwork to have Sage placed in a psychiatric ward. On Sage's second day there, Carmen and Cindy visited. Sage apologized and said he loved them. His mood, however, darkened when he found out they were holding him for seventy-two hours. Opioid withdrawal turned into rage, and a counselor quickly ended the visit. As Carmen and Cindy were leaving, Sage said through tears, "Dad, I'm sorry. I don't want to be like this. Please help me."

Sage's death inspired Carmen to help others, and the one thing he knew about addiction was stigma. He had tried to hide Sage's ordeal, including forbidding him from participating in a video about his addiction. A couple of months after forming Sage's Army, Carmen staged a rally outside of the Westmoreland County Courthouse. He told the crowd of 300 people that he would be damned if he stayed silent any longer and railed against the prescribing practices that filled the streets and medicine cabinets with pills.

Things moved faster than Carmen ever anticipated—and people took notice. Carmen found this out in 2014 when he returned to Hempfield High School, his alma mater, to address an auditorium filled with parents. He retreated to the teacher's lounge shortly before he was to take the stage to work through his nerves. As he made his way back to the auditorium, he turned a corner and froze. A woman flanked by two men wearing earbuds walked straight toward him. Kathleen Kane, the state attorney general, introduced herself. She called him "Mr. Capozzi." *Mr. Capozzi?* Carmen almost looked around to see if his dad was behind him.

"What you're doing here is amazing," she told him. "We need the grassroots. We need your voice. If you ever need anything call me." Carmen stood there stunned, even after she left.

These types of things continued happening as Carmen advocated through Sage's Army. He met with Gary Tennis, head of the state Department of Drug and Alcohol Programs, in Harrisburg and showed him Sage's senior picture. Tennis had a son born on the same day as Sage. He and Carmen cried together. Tennis later appointed Carmen to the state Drug and Alcohol Advisory Council.

Perhaps even more significant to Carmen was what happened one day in Pittsburgh. Walking toward the Allegheny County Courthouse, he asked a woman for directions. She asked if he was an attorney because of his suit. More of a T-shirt and jeans kind of guy, Carmen laughed and said he was speaking at an opioid epidemic hearing. He told her about Sage and how he tries break the stigma of addiction. The woman started crying. She told Carmen that she was a recovering heroin addict. "Wow," she said, "nobody's ever stuck up for me before." Carmen slipped a green Sage's Army bracelet off his right wrist and gave it to her.

POWER IN FORGIVENESS

The verdicts that came in felt like a punch to the gut. Not guilty, not guilty, not guilty. Carmen stared ahead in disbelief. "No, no, no, no..." he said to himself over and over inside of a Westmoreland County courtroom. He'd endured three days of a trial that forced him to relive Sage's death, and he refused to accept the jury's decision.

"You're going to pay," he shouted at twenty-two-year-old Kyland Napper, whom prosecutors alleged sold the fatal batch of heroin to Sage two-and-a-half years earlier. "You killed my son and you f***ing know it! You're going to f***ing pay some day!"

The rage that ricocheted off the wood-paneled walls was something that Carmen tried to bury over the previous two years. He told people at his church that he intended to show Napper forgiveness. He even requested an unorthodox punishment while meeting with the Westmoreland County district attorney's office prior to Napper's preliminary hearing. A recent amendment to the state crimes code gave prosecutors the latitude to pursue stiff sentences for those convicted of dealing drugs that resulted in death. Sage's mother wanted a life sentence for Napper, who was already doing a five- to ten-year stretch for previous drug-related convictions.

Carmen asked for five years with one stipulation: Napper spend the final year of his sentence living with Carmen and working for him. Everyone looked at him as if he'd lost his mind. Tony Marcocci, the longtime Westmoreland County detective, told Carmen that Napper was an unrepentant drug dealer and that he wasn't going to change him. "He has a heart, right?" Carmen said. "I want him to wake up every day and see the life that my son had. If that don't change him, he's all yours."

All of that mercy and forgiveness evaporated when he heard the verdicts for the homicide and drug possession charges. Several sheriff's deputies restrained Carmen as he shouted at Napper. Carmen knew one of them, and they hugged and cried. "He killed my kid," Carmen said.

Outside of the courtroom family members hugged Carmen. He finally left the courthouse with his father's arm draped around his shoulders. "Dad, I failed," Carmen said crying. "I failed everybody. I failed Westmoreland County. We were going to be the first drug conviction by death. I failed us." Carmen Sr. pulled him tight. "You failed nobody," he told his son. "You stood up when nobody else would, and others are going to follow."

When Carmen got to his truck, Nick Carozza, one of Sage's friends, and a sheriff's deputy were waiting to make sure he was okay. On the drive home, Carmen was in another world, trapped by verdicts that he expected to bring some combination of justice and closure. Nick, who had been with Sage the night before he died, finally broke the silence. "Carm, what the hell's going through your head, man?" he said. "Your wheels are spinning." Then something happened that probably surprised Nick more than the courtroom outburst. Carmen said he had to forgive Kyland Napper, for himself as much as for Napper. The rage that engulfed him earlier would destroy him if he didn't douse it with forgiveness.

That night, at the end of the second worst day of his life, he prayed for Kyland Napper. He prayed they would meet one day for something bigger than an apology.

A year later, Carmen addressed around 250 inmates at a state prison in Somerset. He talked about the trial and how he had to leave the courtroom when pictures of Sage's body were shown during testimony. He talked to the group about forgiveness and how doing so ultimately set him free.

Afterward one convicted felon after another approached Carmen to tell him how sorry they were about his son and how much respect they had for him for telling his story. Some asked what they could do to help after they got out of prison. As soon as he got in his truck with another speaker, Jessica McCaffrey, tears started streaming down his face.

"Jess, that's my prayer every night," he said. "For God to come into Kyland Napper's heart and someday come back to me and say, 'How can I help?'"

* * *

Carmen experienced a *saudade* moment in 2017.

It came after he received an email from a woman who sat on the board of one of the largest unions in Pennsylvania and had heard him speak. The union wanted to donate money from its annual fundraiser to Sage's Army. The fundraiser took place in the Poconos in eastern Pennsylvania, and Carmen and Cindy attended a live auction where they were introduced to over 700 people. One stranger after another told them how Sage's Army had inspired them. The show of support overwhelmed Carmen. He quietly left and went back to his hotel room to cry.

Carmen returned the next morning to address the group and was so nervous that he barely ate breakfast. Carmen shared his story for forty-five minutes. The organizers later brought him back onto the stage and presented him with a $12,000 check for Sage's Army.

"It was one of those moments when you want to smile and cry at the same time," Carmen said.

He has had countless of those since starting Sage's Army.

One time, a man hugged Carmen after he told his story at Hot Metal Bridge Church in Pittsburgh. He gave him a bag filled with coins for Sage's Army. It wasn't $12,000, but the $100 the coins added up to was more than that in one sense. The man was homeless, and the money he turned over was all that he had.

To Carmen, it was another nudge to keep going, to keep pushing back against what had taken his son. Sage's Army developed into one of the most prominent grassroots organizations in the state and offers a variety of services. It places addicts in treatment facilities, sponsors support groups for families impacted by addiction and spreads awareness on the opioid epidemic.

Carmen went at everything at such a breakneck pace that he straddled a line between being on fire and burning himself out. At one point, Cindy warned him that he was spreading himself too thin. "Yeah," he said in response, "like a farmer spreading manure on his fields to fertilize the seeds." The joke didn't amuse Cindy. Several people told him the same thing after he posted the joke on his Facebook page.

A couple of days later he woke up early to his cell phone dinging. He checked the inbox on his Facebook page and saw a message. It was from a farmer in North Dakota. He'd watched a video, "Hope after Heroin," which featured Carmen, while riding his tractor. It so moved him that he planned to watch the video with his eleven- and nine-year-old children and start a conversation with them about addiction.

It was a sign, affirmation from above. From God. From Sage. He laid in bed and cried. "Happy birthday, Carm," he said softly to himself on his forty-ninth birthday.

It was another one of what Carmen calls "God moments," and it provided more fuel for his relentless drive. But grief that he never fully dealt with lurked below the surface. It caught up with Carmen when he was in Harrisburg in early 2018 for parent/coach training sessions. He broke down after a meditation exercise, and it felt like day one all over again. The pain of losing Sage was still so intense.

Upon returning home, he started seeing a therapist for post-traumatic stress disorder (PTSD) and suffered a similar breakdown in one of his first sessions. The loss of control, similar to what happened in Harrisburg, unnerved him. The therapist told him to let it out, that it was part of the grieving process. That process is something with which Carmen still struggles.

Carmen Capozzi speaks to a group at a
Greensburg restaurant.

"I think part of my grief is I don't know how to be happy," he said.
"You know how you wake up on a Saturday, and you're driving down
the road in a nice clean truck, and everything is perfect? I don't have
those moments, those moments of pure happiness where there's nothing wrong. I'll be driving down the road and think, *There's no reason
why you should be sad. There's no reason why you should be depressed.
There's nothing wrong today. Everything is good.* But it's hard."

He paused and said, "Grief sucks, man."

AN UNLIKELY ABETTOR

PATH TO CRISIS

A serious car accident in 2009 changed Christine Ackerman's life. Her back hurt so bad even after a lengthy stay in the hospital that she couldn't stand for more than ten minutes at a time. At the supermarket she often knelt, pretending that she was getting something from a bottom shelf when she was just resting.

She initially managed the pain with Vicodin. Even that made Christine uneasy because she didn't want to become addicted to it. She later met with a pain specialist and a pharmaceutical representative. They switched her medication from three Vicodin to six Opana a day.

Christina was skeptical of Opana, an opioid analgesic. But she reluctantly agreed to try it after the pharmaceutical rep assured her that she would not become hooked on Opana since she was using it to relieve pain.

"And I believed her," Christine said. "I started on this medication, and off to hell I went."

She quickly became addicted to Opana, which the Food and Drug Administration pulled off the market in 2018 because the risks outweighed the benefits. Six months after she started taking Opana, she was shooting it. Christine, never a drug user, morphed into someone she didn't know, seemingly overnight. She eventually moved to fentanyl, an opioid much more potent than heroin, and her addiction almost killed her. She overdosed sixteen times. Six times she needed Narcan to save her life.

"Things went south so quick," Christine said. "I would say to myself, 'OK, this is the last time I'm going to do this.' Then an hour later, 'OK, now this is the last time I'm going to do it.' Then an hour later, 'OK, *this* is the last time.'"

Nothing better illustrates the rabbit hole of addiction than the line Christine would draw for herself—and then move it because she needed a fix. The North Huntingdon resident has been in recovery for two years. Her story raises the larger question of the roles the pharmaceutical and medical communities played in catalyzing the opioid epidemic, intentionally or not.

Sam Quinones, author of *Dreamland,* a seminal and chilling book on the epidemic, chronicled the alarming rise of opiate use in the United States. Quinones wrote that heroin flooded the nation as a critical pivot in the medical community occurred. A resulting confluence helped release an insatiable demand for opiates.

In 1980, a precursor to the opioid epidemic occurred when the World Health Organization (WHO) declared that pain relief is a basic human right and that doctors should do whatever it takes to treat pain. That same year, Dr. Hershel Jick wrote a letter to the esteemed *New England Journal of Medicine* highlighting a study that he and an assistant conducted. They monitored hospital patients who were given narcotics to treat pain and found that only four of the 12,000 participants became addicted to the medication.

The study was very controlled, the letter said, from the setting to the doses given to patients. And Jick did not elaborate on specifics of the study, such as its length or dosages given to patients. According to *Dreamland,* Jick never intended for the letter to be construed as a breakthrough in treating pain with opioids.

But, as Quinones writes, Jick's findings gathered momentum and eventually turned into gospel to many in the medical community. Even *Time* magazine ran with it, citing the Jick letter in a 2001 story as a "landmark study" that quelled fears about the link between opioids used to treat pain and opioid addiction. Of course, none of this happened in a vacuum.

In 1996, the American Pain Society (APS) advocated adding pain as a fifth vital sign along with body temperature, pulse, blood pressure, and respiratory rate, so it could be treated properly. Treatment of pain was deemed such a priority that it put pressure on doctors and hospitals. Pharmaceutical companies, meanwhile, developed and marketed opioids that relieved pain, making it easier for doctors to prescribe them for patients who were suffering. All of it led to oversteering the car in treating pain.

The perverse irony, as Quinones writes, is that the exact opposite of what Jick wrote about in his letter to the *New England Journal of Medicine* happened. Pain medication wasn't dispensed in controlled doses, and most patients weren't closely monitored in hospitals. Instead, patients took prescription medication home where they monitored taking it themselves.

Not coincidentally, prescription pain medication overdose deaths soared. They increased 400 percent from 1999–2010 for women, according to the American Society of Addiction Medicine (ASAM), and 237 percent for men during that period. Even those spikes did not curtail the use of prescription pain medication. In 2012, according to ASAM, 259 million opioid prescriptions were written, clearly putting some culpability for the opioid epidemic on the medical community.

"The blame is at every level," said Dr. John Gallagher, who presides over the Pennsylvania Medical Society Opioid Task Force. "Patients wanted to be pain free. Doctors wanted to keep patients happy. Drug companies wanted to sell drugs."

Gallagher said pain is a reality of life and that most people can still function properly while dealing with it. "People have to recognize they can't be pain free," he said. "Doctors have to realize that we have to be more cautious."

Indeed, scores of people I interviewed told me that they have been prescribed medication for something analogous to killing an ant with a gun. I heard countless examples of people receiving a prescription for

Percocet, a narcotic that contains oxycodone, or something stronger following his having a tooth pulled.

Westmoreland County Coroner Ken Bacha said after shoulder surgery, he was given a prescription for ninety Oxycontin tablets, a powerful narcotic originally manufactured to treat end-of-life pain for cancer patients. Bacha didn't ask for any medication, took one of the Oxycontin pills, and threw the rest away.

Dave Lettrich said he simply wanted Motrin after major knee surgery and was denied that request. The reason he was prescribed opioids following surgery? Medical personnel didn't want to get a call from Lettrich in the middle of the night complaining that he was in too much pain.

The Latrobe resident still shakes his head at having opioids prescribed to him against his wishes.

"It's ridiculous," said Lettrich, who ministers to homeless addicts through his nonprofit organization, Bridge to the Mountains. "We've killed half a million people with opioids. What sane nation knows we've killed half a million people, but it's necessary to keep society comfortable? At what point do you say, 'This is freakin' insanity?'"

It is getting better in a better-late-than-never kind of way.

According to Gallagher, opioid prescriptions have dropped between 15 to 20 percent nationally due, in part, to prescription monitoring databases implemented by individual states. This deters people from "doctor shopping," which is going from physician to physician to get prescriptions for pain medication, since a person's prescription history can be easily accessed.

Gallagher said Pennsylvania is doing more to educate people on prescription medication and that the state has opened return centers for unused opiate medication. It's better for opiates to be turned over to people who can properly dispose of them rather than leave them in a medicine cabinet where kids can get to them, Gallagher said.

Slowly shutting off the opioids spigot, however, has resulted in the unintended consequence of driving up overdose deaths. People who have been abusing prescription pain medication will turn to illegal opiates if they can't get pills, Gallagher said. The danger that poses has increased exponentially due to the rise of fentanyl and carfentanil. In Westmoreland County, 138 of the 193 people who died from overdoses in 2017 had fentanyl in their system, according to the coroner's office.

Bacha said medical experts warned him that overdose deaths would spike as the supply of prescription medication decreased.

"And that's exactly what happened as our statistics show," he said.

Bacha doesn't expect overdose deaths in Westmoreland County to plateau for years based on projections from epidemiologists and his own experiences. Gallagher said that only makes Westmoreland County like the rest of the country.

"It's taken thirty years to get where we are now," Gallagher said. "Anybody that thinks we're going to fix the problem in the next five years is crazy."

* * *

Easier access to prescription pain medication and the resulting gateway to heroin abuse makes a good narrative. But to Dr. Eric Kocian, it is too simplistic.

Kocian, a criminology professor at St. Vincent College in Latrobe, reached that conclusion after conducting a 2017 study with Dr. John Lewis, a criminology professor at the University of Indiana at Pennsylvania. The two interviewed 158 addicts serving time at the Westmoreland County Prison. None interviewed moved to heroin if they took pain medication as prescribed and largely abstained from drinking and drug use before prescription pain medication entered the equation. Only one of the 158 addicts interviewed went strictly from abusing pain medication to heroin abuse.

That is not to discount the link between prescription medication and heroin. But to Kocian and Lewis, it's often more of a circuitous route than a direct one since almost everyone in their study drank and used marijuana or cocaine at an early age before moving up the opiate chain to heroin.

"We were shocked at the number of drugs that people were experimenting with before they even started touching heroin and/or pain pills," Kocian said. "It's just one small sample of southwestern Pennsylvania but we found a lot more drug behavior before pain pills."

Blaming the ubiquity of pain pills on the opioid epidemic "misses the point," Kocian said. "If opiate medication by itself steered people to illegal opiates, the epidemic would be much worse because of how frequently legal opiates are still used to treat pain."

That belief seems to be at odds with the fact that eighty percent of heroin users first abused prescription medication, according to ASAM. But that statistic doesn't reveal what those heroin users were into before they started abusing prescription medication.

Kocian and Lewis's study provides some context to that statistic.

"It's like a baseball lineup," Kocian said. "Number eight in the order is prescription medication. Number nine is heroin. If you just focus on those batters in the order, what about the runners (ahead of them) that are getting on base? To win the game, you want to hold off on getting those people on base as long as you can."

Kocian's baseball metaphor illustrates his belief that the opioid epidemic may be more tied to early drug use than anything else.

"As heartless as it sounds, if you gambled on who's going do to heroin and who's not, my question isn't, 'Do they use prescription medication?' My question is, 'When did they start using illegal drugs?'" he said. "If someone started using marijuana, my guess is eventually they're going to move onto something more serious."

Christine Ackerman is an outlier to the Kocian and Lewis study. She *is* the suburban mom who never had a drinking problem or drug history but became addicted to pain medication. That doesn't make her any less of a cautionary tale or minimize the dangers of prescription medication.

The measures Christine takes to maintain sobriety is proof of the latter.

She attends 12-step meetings and is part of the Peer Nursing Assistance Program (PNAP), which monitors addicts and subjects them to safeguards such as random drug testing and counseling. Christine's not sure she will return to nursing because of the proximity to medicine (although she may go into the recovery aspect of nursing).

No matter where her career leads, Christine has decided to stay with PNAP for the rest of her life. That means paying for her own drug tests, checking in with the organization every day, and never again touching a drink.

Christine has already spent over $50,000 on PNAP, but it will be well worth it if it keeps her in recovery.

"It's not a punishment," Christine said. "I crossed a line in life, and I don't want to do this again. If I (relapse) I want to catch it early and treat it because this doesn't go away. I'm trying to save myself. I'm trying to save my family. I just want to live."

TRAGEDY OF RELAPSE

Dr. Jonathan Han doesn't spare his own profession when discussing root causes of the opioid epidemic.

"The medical community helped create this by overprescribing opioids. Pharma really pushed it and lied about how safe they were when most doctors in the community knew they weren't," Han said. "Now that we're in this predicament, they need to step up to the plate and help fix it."

Nothing gives more weight to this scathing indictment than the link between pain medication and heroin for four out of five heroin addicts.

What about when that works in reverse with tragic consequences? Sharon Stinebiser lost both of her sons in a seven-hour period to fentanyl overdoses in 2016. A part of her dad died, too, when Joshaua Gunther and Dylan Fisher passed, since he had been like a father to them. Sharon will never know if Dylan was so distraught over losing his older brother and best friend that he committed suicide or simply shot fentanyl to numb the pain, even though he wasn't into drugs. After their deaths, Sharon found out that Josh was buying drugs online, something that still boggles her mind.

"Nine years clean and then (relapsing)," she said of Josh. "I never thought that would happen."

Brothers and best friends Josh Gunther and Dylan Fisher. Photo courtesy of Sharon Stinebiser

She traces the relapse she never saw coming to a car accident that left Josh with six broken ribs and on a morphine drip. The accident kept Josh from working and he routinely put in sixty- or seventy-hour work weeks at DeLallo Italian Marketplace in Jeannette. In addition to the morphine, Josh was given a prescription for Oxycontin to help with the pain, Sharon said.

She doesn't blame doctors or the hospital as much as she does the system. The questionnaire Josh filled out when he was admitted to the hospital asked if he was currently using opiates. It didn't ask if he had *previously* used opiates—a critical and possibly deadly distinction.

Pat Williams' son had a similar experience. It forced Pat to add a chapter to his book, *Returning to the Light,* that he never wanted to write. Luke Williams died from a fentanyl overdose on July 15, 2017. Like Josh, Luke hid his drug use after relapsing. Like Sharon, Pat traced the relapse to opiates Luke received in a hospital. Luke hurt his back on July 4, 2016, after attempting a backflip on a trampoline. At Indiana Hospital, he received Tylenol for the pain. But he was transferred to another hospital, which Pat declined to name, where he was given opiates despite repeated warnings that Luke was a recovering addict.

"At the hospital, the first thing I did was go to the nurses and tell them that Luke was nine years clean and not to give him any addictive drugs," Pat said. "His fiancée told every medical professional she saw not to give him narcotics. The local NA group did the same thing. They were told at least ten times, no narcotics."

The warnings were ignored, and Luke was placed on a morphine drip to ease the pain. He left the hospital with a prescription for Oxycontin, which Luke's fiancée ripped up in front of the doctor.

That was the beginning of Luke's downfall. Pat places a lot of the blame for that spiral on the since-debunked medical opinion that the body can differentiate when an opioid is used for pain treatment and when it is taken to get high.

"You don't give painkillers to an addict. That's what killed my son," he said. "An addict is addicted for life. You can never let your guard down."

Nothing better illustrated the dichotomy of Luke the person and Luke the addict than the day he died. Luke had promised to babysit his fiancée's daughter but never showed up. His fiancée fumed as she cleaned the house until she found a letter from Luke. Her anger melted as she read the four-page letter Luke had written about their lives together and how he'd always love her. She went to Luke's apartment and found him dead from an overdose.

"After they found him," Pat said, "her daughter turned to her and said, 'I guess it's just you and me again.'"

Pat still has many questions that will probably never get answered. Did Luke get "too close to the fire" in working as a certified recovery specialist? Did he take it too personally when someone he counseled fatally overdosed? How was he able to hide his relapse for so long?

Pat is certain that the hospital that gave Luke opiates set him on an inexorable path to his death at thirty-three.

When we met, Pat was strongly considering a wrongful death lawsuit—not for money but for awareness so another family doesn't have to suffer what he and his family have in losing Luke.

Pat honors Luke's memory by spreading his story, especially the uplifting part of it. He counsels addicts in prison and tells them how Luke made it back from the depths. He speaks out against stigma but also wrestles with questions of whether he enabled Luke's earlier drug use because he didn't take a harder stance and throw him out of the house.

"The whole thing is like a Shakespearean tragedy," Pat said. "We're doing well only because of our faith."

Pat finds comfort and purpose in stories he hears about Luke and the impact he had on others. Shortly after Luke passed, Pat gave one of Luke's Narcotics Anonymous milestone coins to a friend of Luke's who also struggles with addiction. That friend later told Pat that he was in the process of buying heroin when he reached into his pocket and touched the coin by chance.

It stopped him from making the buy. He instead attended a 12-step meeting.

WHY NARCAN IS COMPLICATED

A mid-December day in 2017 produced a biting cold that had me wanting to stay in Rev. Clark Kerr's office. Kerr and I met at Latrobe Presbyterian Church an hour before the latest public prayer gathering he organized to bring awareness to the opioid epidemic.

We talked about a number of things in his cozy office, including Duke basketball (he is a graduate), golf (he has several pictures of Arnold Palmer among his various photos), and Southern California.

Kerr was born in Latrobe but spent six of his formative years in Southern California before his family moved back to the area. He compared heroin users to surfers he grew up watching, trying to catch the perfect wave. Kerr exuded a calm that called to mind SoCal, but he made it clear that he was as mad as he was frustrated about the opioid epidemic. He directed much of his anger at big pharma and the liberal prescribing of pain medication.

He has channeled that anger into work with other churches and helped stage prayer rallies to bring awareness to the epidemic. Kerr strategically scheduled the rally I was attending behind the church's red brick building, so motorists passing by on Main Street would see it. Maybe someone in need would see it and ask for help. It was a tactic respected church leaders like Kerr could do to fight the epidemic.

As we finished our chat, Kerr said he'd recently attended a training session on Narcan, which reverses the effects of an overdose. He showed me a small spray bottle and said, "The last thing I ever want to do is have to use it."

He almost did less than a half hour later.

During the prayer rally, a teenage boy fell to the ground. A couple of his friends helped him to his feet, but clearly something wasn't right. Kerr asked his friends if he'd overdosed. Though unsteady on his feet, the young man claimed that he was fine, and he simply hadn't eaten anything. (I later found out that he had indeed shot up before the rally and was only fourteen years old.)

Rev. Clark Kerr leads a prayer rally outside of Latrobe Presbyterian Church.

This is where we are, I thought, as a couple of people walked the boy home: ministers armed with Narcan. And with good reason.

"I couldn't imagine what our (deaths statistics) would be without Narcan," Westmoreland County Coroner Ken Bacha said.

Four months after Kerr introduced me to Narcan, a diatribe that generated headlines also shined a light on how polarizing the life-saving drug can be.

Don Smith of the Lloydsville Volunteer Fire Department offered a scathing indictment of Narcan on a national firefighters' website. "Worthless junkies can just die," he wrote. "They made the choice to stick the needle in their arm." The post was later deleted, and the Lloydsville Fire Department suspended Smith and issued a statement rebuking his position.

Smith, however, refused to back down the following day on a KDKA Channel 2 report, and I wondered how many people agreed with him. To get a small sample size, I read the *Tribune-Review's* online story two days after it was posted. The fifteen-plus comments largely praised Smith. Some wrote that the action taken against him was driven by political correctness.

One person posted, "F*ck the junkies. Waste of $$$. Go Don!!!"

Narcan, as it turns out, is complicated. Just like everything else when it comes to the opioid epidemic.

* * *

Bree Swarmer is squarely on the fault line when it comes to the Narcan debate. She needed it twenty-three times during her addiction, which was once so severe that her mom set aside money for her funeral. She often cursed the police officers who saved her with Narcan for robbing her of a good buzz. One time, she swung at officers after they revived her.

Greg Powell gave first responders a different problem one time after he overdosed. He had to be restrained in the ambulance as it drove to a hospital because he kept trying to jump out of a moving vehicle. Greg was disoriented after first responders revived him and became panicked when he thought of the drugs that police would find in his car.

Like Greg, Bree shakes her head at such behavior.

"That's the insanity that comes with drug addiction," she said.

To Bree, the same insanity prevails among those who rail against the widespread use of Narcan and say addicts should only get so many doses of it before they are cut off. The New Castle resident drew on an analogy to illustrate her point.

"Say you have a woman in an abusive relationship with her husband. On the fourth call to police that her husband's beating her, they don't go because they told her before she should have left?" Bree said. "So, you just let her get killed? That's the exact same thing."

At the very least, it treads on dangerous ground.

"I understand their frustration," Westmoreland County Commissioner Gina Cerilli said of first responders who continually save the same addicts with Narcan. "But we're not God. We can't tell a person, 'Oh, you only get three chances.'"

Cerilli prioritized the opioid epidemic when she ran for office in 2015. She views Narcan not as enabling addicts but keeping them alive, so they can eventually get help. She cited an example of an addict who was an acquaintance of her sister. He wrote to Cerilli after she took office and thanked her for keeping attention on the opioid epidemic. He said he was closing in on his second year of sobriety after years of bouncing between rehabilitation facilities and jail.

"It sometimes takes people more than three chances to get their life back on track," Cerilli said.

Jeff Held understands both sides of the Narcan argument. Held worked as a paramedic for more than fifteen years in Armstrong County before taking a different job. He was vomited on and swung at after administering Narcan. Held never hesitated to save someone who'd overdosed but did have the unsympathetic mindset of "If they live, they live. If they die, they die." Held said many veteran paramedics probably have that mentality because of their experiences.

His view on Narcan started to change in 2014 while he was mayor of Apollo Borough and dealt with drugs on a different front. A pair of drive-by shootings in a quiet neighborhood and a major drug bust in an apartment building behind his house spurred Held to seek answers. A series of meetings with law enforcement officials and people in the community led to the formation of Residents Against Illicit Drugs (R.A.I.D.) in 2016.

The nonprofit organization spreads awareness and promotes education. It also provides support to those who are struggling with addiction. Held told me about one call he received from a mother asking for help with her son. She'd found a bag of white powder in his bedroom. Held advised her to get Narcan.

Held said the family had Narcan for only four hours when the father needed it to revive his son from an overdose. Held saw the family a couple of weeks later, and it had not been ripped apart by death. He thought to himself, "We're making a difference."

That experience cemented his reversal on Narcan.

"I decided my ingrained thought process was outdated, irrational, and just plain stupid," Held said. "If Narcan saves somebody's brother, sister, mother, son, isn't that worth it? As long as they are breathing, they have a chance at recovery. Sometimes it's going to be the sixteenth time, and they get it and turn themselves around. I've lost a lot of friends because they don't think I should be giving Narcan training to people."

* * *

Mike Stangroom is also on the front lines of the opioid epidemic. A paramedic and a police officer, he has almost fifty years of combined services in those fields.

Stangroom runs the Rostraver-West Newton Emergency Medical Services (EMS). Prior to the opioid epidemic, his crew might have used Narcan a couple of times a month. And that was in a bad month.

And now? I asked him that question in March 2018.

"Every single day."

Stangroom said those words slowly to punctuate how weary it has made him. Recently, one of Stangroom's crew revived a fifty-three-year-old woman with Narcan after she overdosed in her yard. They took her to Mon-Valley Hospital, where she gave the emergency room staff a hard time. She refused treatment and signed a waiver acknowledging she left the hospital against medical advice.

A crew was called back to the same house later that night, this time for a fifty-one-year-old man who overdosed. The man died after resuscitation efforts failed. He was the brother of the woman who had overdosed earlier.

"Why in the hell, if you just almost died, would you give it to your brother?" Stangroom said. "What power does this drug have over people?"

What frustrates Stangroom and other first responders is they often feel handcuffed in the fight against the opioid epidemic. They can recommend treatment but cannot compel someone to seek help even if they save the same person multiple times. That leaves them to deal with the other end of the law that aims to curb fatalities by allowing anyone to call emergency responders after an overdose without any legal consequences.

Westmoreland Single County Authority (SCA) is trying to bridge the gap between saving a person with Narcan and getting them long-term help.

Liz Comer of SCA, which receives and disperses state funds for drug and alcohol treatment, oversees Leave Narcan Behind. Started in 2017, the program provides participating Emergency Medical Services with Narcan kits and Narcan training and release forms that are returned to SCA. The release forms are offered to people who have been given Narcan to reverse an overdose. If they sign the form, SCA will promptly follow up with a certified recovery specialist or a drug-and-alcohol case manager to try to get that person into treatment.

Randy Highlands, the director of Jeannette EMS, is hopeful Leave Narcan Behind will make a difference but isn't overly optimistic. As Highlands said, if someone is telling you to get the hell out of their house after you revive them, how are you going to get them to sign something that invites more intrusion?

"It's another tool in the box, but it's not going to solve the big picture problem," he said.

Highlands, who has worked in emergency response since the 1980s, has similar reservations about making Narcan so readily available.

"I'll probably be called an SOB for saying it, but sometimes I question putting Narcan in the hands of the public because we're enabling addicts," he said. "Then you have the six-year-old boy who's allergic to bee stings, and we're charging them $600, $700 dollars for epinephrine but we're giving Narcan away. This kid's throat closes up through something he didn't choose to do, and here's another person who chooses to stick that needle in his arm. Maybe that's a bad way to look at it."

Highlands said his own ambivalence toward Narcan doesn't affect how he approaches his job.

"Nobody wants to see anybody die," he said. "We are in this to save lives."

But saving lives costs money and ambulance centers like the one Highlands runs have limited budgets. They rely on donations and money that is generated through nonemergency services, such as transportation from a hospital to a rehabilitation center. Narcan is provided to EMS centers by hospitals. But EMS centers don't always get paid for transporting an overdosed person to the hospital.

What is more exasperating to Highlands than the hospital trips that aren't paid for because a person doesn't have health insurance is what often takes place in the home where they are called. Highlands has countless examples of saving someone who overdosed only to be told to get the hell out of their house since they didn't call for an ambulance. Highlands and his team also encounter addicts who, upon waking up after getting revived with Narcan, insist that they didn't take anything and refuse further treatment.

If EMTs don't know how much of a drug someone has taken, they don't know if that person will lose consciousness again after the Narcan wears off. More than once, Highlands has returned to a house or apartment he had been to earlier because an addict insisted they didn't take anything but needed more Narcan.

What bothers Highlands most is the sheer terror he sees from other people when he treats someone, especially children.

"That's when the father in me really comes out," said Highlands, who has three kids. "The look of fear in these kids' faces, it's hard to describe. And rather than hug these kids and cry with them, I take it the other way and go crazy on the individual like, 'These are your kids! These kids don't deserve this!' Sometimes they get it. Sometimes they just don't care. It's very frustrating and none of us signed up for this when we started."

James Bumar can attest to how much the opioid epidemic has changed the emergency response landscape.

Bumar spent almost thirty-five years in law enforcement before retiring as Latrobe chief of police in September 2018. Latrobe police officers carry Narcan, and prior to retiring, Bumar changed the department's policy of handing drugs seized during an arrest. Because heroin is so often laced with fentanyl and carfentanil, the department no longer conducts field tests on drugs seized during arrests. Instead, they're sent to a laboratory because it is simply too dangerous for officers to risk exposure to lethal opiates.

What Bumar advocates for Narcan has both a carrot-and-stick component. He knows from the failure of the War on Drugs in the 1980s, that law enforcement can't just arrest our way out of the problem. He teamed with Rev. Clark Kerr and others to spread awareness and also took the approach that police aren't just going to arrest addicts but try to help them.

What he advocates for Narcan has a carrot-and-stick component to it. It mandates that someone needing Narcan has to enter a program that includes addiction education and possibly treatment. If the person completes the program, they aren't charged for the Narcan. If they don't complete the program, they must pay for the Narcan.

That thinking reflects the biggest problem first responders have when it comes to their role in the opioid epidemic. They are essentially fighting it with one arm tied behind their back since they can't do more than reverse an overdose with Narcan and hope for the best.

"We have the repeat customers who are not learning," Stangroom said. "I'm a Christian and I'm here to help people, but it's frustrating to work your ass off to save a person, and three days later it's the same scenario. It's a bad, bad situation right now. We are losing the war."

AN ADDICTION CULTURE?

The road to Teen Challenge in Cheswick snakes its way up a steep hill, cutting a path through cascading trees, a few of which have no hunting signs. It's a place where someone could easily get lost, and it is where Justin Drish, thirty-two years old, found himself. The long and winding road is a perfect metaphor for his path to recovery.

I met Justin at a Primanti Brothers restaurant that is only a couple of miles from Teen Challenge but seems like a world away. The figurative distance was the same for the person I chatted with that day and the one who had gone to Teen Challenge almost six-and-a-half years earlier when he was out of options.

The dramatic, life-saving changes Justin eventually made could be distilled to something he said without a hint of levity.

"My mother leaves her purse in the same room with me now," he said.

To say Justin lived a hard life before achieving long-term recovery is an understatement. The Elizabeth native sold and used drugs in high school. He got into opiates after he broke his ankle while on break from a lucrative but demanding job in demolition in his early twenties. Justin started taking Vicodin for the pain and later turned to Oxycontin. He eventually returned home to Elizabeth after hurting his knee on the job, and his Oxy dependence became so intense that he cashed out his 401k plan even though he was also selling pills to support his habit.

And yet, in one sense, he still didn't see himself as an addict because he was only abusing prescription pain medication.

"My perception was if you were doing heroin, you were a straight scumbag," Justin said with wry laugh. "And here I was doing pain pills throughout the day."

The need for those pills inevitably led to a point of no return. It happened when he and his friends ran out of prescriptions and had trouble finding pain pills on the streets. Heroin was easily accessible. Justin fooled himself into thinking he could do heroin just one time to get him through a rough patch and then go back to pain pills. It was easy to convince himself of that while he was dealing with opiate withdrawal.

"It is the worst feeling I've felt in my life," he said. "It feels like your bones are exploding from the inside out."

The devious economics of addiction kept Justin from returning to pain pills. Heroin simply provided more bang for his buck, and his life predictably imploded.

Justin, who made good money in his early twenties, ended up homeless and living in his car. He stole so often from his parents that they finally gave him an ultimatum that landed him at Teen Challenge, an all-men's facility. A month into his stay, one of his best friends committed suicide because of heroin withdrawal. His parents didn't tell him the news because they feared he would try to leave the program.

Justin completed a four-month stint at Cheswick and then moved to the ten-month part of the program near Harrisburg.

The faith-based approach worked so well for him that he returned to the Cheswick facility as an intern. Eventually, he joined the staff as a counselor. Justin, who barely graduated from high school, earned a bachelor's degree in psychology and has been accepted into a master's program at Waynesburg University. He plans to study addiction there and has already done extensive research on the topic.

"We have a culture of addiction. It's not just heroin," he said. "We are a society that has to have what we want now, which opens up the door for something like (opiate use) to explode, and it did. We have a pill for everything. From a young age we are producing addicts."

In fact, Justin traces the addiction that almost cost him everything to the medication he started taking in kindergarten for attention deficit hyperactivity disorder (ADHD). He does not fault his parents for giving him the medication after his diagnosis. But he is convinced that he is the product of a culture in which medicine is too often used to address perceived behavior or mood issues.

"I was told I had a learning disorder and that I couldn't concentrate, that I had to be in special classes," Justin said. "So in my young mind, I have a problem. I take a pill and that solves the problem."

That figurative pill led to problems because of the mindset instilled in him at an early age.

He started using marijuana and alcohol at the age of thirteen because it made him feel better. It led him to engage in risky behavior that, in teen years, can have disastrous long-term consequences. That is why Justin goes all the way back to his five-year-old self when he talks about himself as a case study in addiction.

"When I put it that I was taking amphetamines for ADHD, it kind of alarms people but we don't hear it talked about like that," Justin said.

As a drug-and-alcohol counselor, he stresses the importance of developing coping skills instead of turning to drugs as an escape.

"Anxiety, depression, and stress are all normal and healthy emotions," Justin said. "When somebody dies, it's okay to feel depressed. Yet we medicate these emotions instead of working through them. Whenever we medicate, we don't know how to deal with life anymore. I think that's what our culture is driving us to do, to have this state of numbness, euphoria, where we shouldn't ever get stressed out."

Justin said there *should* be consequences from poor decisions, which dovetails with the accountability that is one of the foundations of his sobriety.

"You should be stressed out if you're in credit card debt. Why? Because you suck at spending (money)," he said. "It's not your emotions that are unhealthy. It's your behavior that's unhealthy. It's your values that are unhealthy. I see more and more people accepting that they're going to need medication to deal with everyday life. My problem isn't that there aren't legitimate mental issues. It's that I believe everyday normal life has become too medicated and that we're overdiagnosing."

At least one expert agrees with him.

Dr. Allen J. Francis chaired the task force that produced the fourth version of the *Diagnostic and Statistical Manuel of Mental Disorders* but has been critical of the fifth and most current edition, published in 2013. Francis said it includes so many diagnoses that it's leading psychiatry toward treating what is largely normal behavior instead of focusing on legitimate mental-health issues.

Balancing the prevalence of mental illness in the United States with the reality that many psychiatric diagnoses depend largely on what patients say is tricky. Maybe even a slippery slope considering one in five American adults lives with mental illness, according to the National Institute of Mental Health.

I was thinking about a different kind of slope after we left Primanti Brothers and I followed Justin to Teen Challenge. The road never seems to end, and snowbanks had formed on this day at different junctures of the serpentine path. We made it safely to the top, where Justin gave me a quick history lesson. The facility had been a NIKE missile site and was a good place to transmit information if nuclear hostilities broke out during the Cold War.

The remote location is conducive to treating addiction since one of the biggest drawbacks with some drug-and-alcohol treatment facilities is that they are too close to areas where drug dealers linger.

Teen Challenge has several buildings, and the main one includes a chapel with wooden pews and classrooms for meetings. There are also bedrooms with bunk beds and a recreational area where residents can shoot pool or watch TV. An adjacent facility has a kitchen, and there was Christian music playing as Justin and I walked through it.

Teen Challenge has thirty beds and encourages addicts to enroll for the fourteen-month program, the last ten of which are spent in Harrisburg. But it also offers a thirty-day program just to get addicts through the door in the hopes that they will stay with Teen Challenge beyond the initial commitment.

Dave Lewis, director of Teen Challenge's Cheswick center, said that in 2017, twenty-five of the ninety-seven men who entered the thirty-day program advanced to the second stage. That was a promising start since the longer addicts stay in the program, the better their chance of achieving long-term recovery.

"My goal is to get addicts into long-term treatment," Justin said. "Thirty days is just not long enough."

Justin uses himself as an example to those he counsels about the benefits of addressing addiction with a long-range view and program. He completely turned his life around and is married with two kids. He teaches Sunday school at Harvest Bible Chapel in Monroeville and has rebuilt relationships that his addiction all but shredded.

Justin said his descent into heroin started when it was just starting to hit the suburbs. With the prevalence of fentanyl and carfentanil making it more dangerous than ever for addicts, he is lucky to have made it to his thirties.

"By the grace of God, I made it out by the time that stuff started circulating," he said. "With the statistics, it's a miracle that I am here today."

Now the guy who graduated from high school with a 1.3 GPA writes his own papers and embraces learning. He believes in himself, something he couldn't say growing up.

"To me, the ADHD label meant I couldn't concentrate and I wasn't smart," Justin said. "It led me to academic failure."

He learned the hard way that labels carry a lot of power. That's why, even while he still wears a watch that tracks his clean time to the minute, he refuses to label himself an addict.

"I used to be but I'm not defined by that anymore," Justin said.

That is not to say he has relaxed in maintaining sobriety. If anything, he has become more vigilant about it. Justin had the occasional drink after progressing enough in recovery to think it wouldn't cause a relapse. But after weighing its risks, he swore off alcohol.

"Who knows, maybe I am the one in a million who can have a couple of drinks here and there after being a heroin addict," he said. "But I've got kids now. I've got a wife. It just doesn't make sense."

HORRIBLE WAY TO LIVE

He stood on a street corner in the Oakland section of Pittsburgh and contemplated stepping into the lane designated for buses. Those buses go fast, and he figured it was a quick way to free himself from the bonds of addiction. He wasn't thinking about his three young kids or that he still had a good job as a human resources specialist. Two years after becoming addicted to prescription pain medication, Rich Jones had lost all hope.

"I remember having a moment where I thought, 'There never will be enough pills,'" he said.

He had started taking pain medication after getting rear-ended at a red light, and it didn't take long for addiction to overwhelm him. He would get panicky *after* getting a prescription filled because he knew he only had a limited supply of pills.

"I was always terrified that I was going to run out," Rich said. "It's a horrible way to live, and I think that's where the suicidal thinking came in."

Rich is far from that street corner these days and not just because the Stahlstown native lives in South Carolina. Rich is the CEO of Faces and Voices of Recovery (FAVOR), a nonprofit organization that works with more than 20,000 people who are battling addiction or impacted by it.

To many, Rich is an unlikely face of addiction. A 1986 graduate of Ligonier Valley High School, he played on the football and basketball teams and served as the class president. He had a good career, marriage, and life prior to the car accident in his late twenties that sent him to the hospital with head and neck injuries, albeit relatively minor ones.

He left the hospital with 120 Darvocet pills (the FDA banned the opioid used to treat pain in 2010), "and it was game on," Rich said.

It almost turned into game over.

Opiates slapped such a stranglehold on Rich that he soon found himself on that street corner, debating taking his own life. How in the hell had he gotten here? It was both a simple and complicated question.

He burned through money and sometimes stole to feed his addiction. He once ate a handful of pills and got into an accident with his kids in the car. He doctor-shopped and made frequent trips to emergency rooms to get more pills. Yet, there was never enough.

Timing is the only reason he didn't take his opiate addiction to the next level.

"I didn't have the heroin option," Rich said. "It just wasn't around in '98 like it is now. People say they don't understand how these kids (today) can jump to heroin. I understand. I would have done it in a New York minute."

Rich's family helped save him from himself. His wife and mother learned about addiction at a time when there were significantly less opportunities to do so. They set boundaries and refused to enable Rich's behavior. His wife eventually kicked him out of the house. That set Rich on the path to recovery, and he has been helping others for more than a decade in Allegheny and Westmoreland counties and now South Carolina.

"I say all the time that if my family wouldn't have gotten educated, I'd be dead now because I was seriously, seriously suicidal," said Rich, who has been in recovery since 2001.

His story foreshadowed what happened across the country after changing attitudes toward opiates and pain treatment merged to form one of the paths to the opioid epidemic.

"I've learned from doctors and neurologists that certain people have a propensity for opioids. They tend to fit our brain like a puzzle piece," Rich said. "Some take an opioid, and they might end up feeling very, very lethargic or even nauseous. But when I take an opioid, it's a perfect fit. I get energetic and feel like I'm on top of the world. I think I was one those people whose brain was just tailor-made for opioids."

The trouble with this is similar, in one sense, to the existential problem facing football and its link to long-term problems such as depression and dementia. With football, it is almost impossible to know whether someone who absorbs repeated hits to the head is more prone to chronic traumatic encephalopathy (CTE). The same is largely true in determining whether someone is more predisposed to opiate addiction since their brain cannot be extensively studied while still alive.

That makes assessing how individuals will react to opiates a guessing game, even if factors such as family history facilitate educated guesses. What infuriates Rich is his belief that the pharmaceutical industry, like the tobacco industry before it, duped the public on how addictive opiates are even when used to treat pain.

"There's no doubt in my mind that it was intentional marketing and false and misleading advertising," he said. "That's where my frustration goes. I'm not angry toward doctors. I've gotten to know a lot of doctors, and I feel the health-care system is actually part of the solution moving forward."

Rich is trying to be part of that solution. FAVOR educates budding doctors at the University of South Carolina Medical College through a class for third-year medical students that focuses on addiction and recovery. Rich is optimistic that doctors, with growing awareness, are becoming more responsible when prescribing pain medication. That is part of solving the problem.

"But how do we put the horses back in the barn for the people who have already become addicted?" Rich said. "How do we deal with the fact that even if we get rid of all of the prescriptions, we know that heroin, fentanyl, and carfentanil is still going to show up?"

That question is part of what makes the opioid epidemic so complex—and why more people like Rich are needed. He embraces outside of the box thinking and thinks more of it is needed to confront such a confounding issue.

One answer Rich couldn't give me as we talked about the opioid epidemic and what needs to change is what stopped him from stepping off that curb when his pain-pill addiction left him hopeless.

"God, or maybe it was just lack of courage," he said. "I really don't know. It was sort of a fantasy I had, that if this continues, this is my way out. It was no way to live."

What breaks his heart is seeing kids dealing with the despair he experienced as an adult when he was fully developed and had life experiences to draw on as he fought through the adversity.

"Can you imagine what it's like to be the seventeen-year-old popping these pills in the back of the classroom, and all of the sudden he's in that state of mind?" Rich said. "I can't imagine what it would be like to be a teenager or a young adult and be where I was."

* * *

Imagine being in your mid-fifties and you never really drank much and never liked opioid-based medication because it made you sick. You were on Xanax for years but always managed it while raising a daughter as a single mother and working as a court reporter and then a bridal consultant. Then, over two years, you started popping Xanax, a benzodiazepine used to treat anxiety, so frequently that it became an addiction. You finally slit your wrists because you didn't know how else to break free of its suffocating grip.

Joyce Maybach, fifty-nine years old, lived that nightmare before spending almost a year-and-a-half in a rehabilitation facility and then two recovery houses. By the time she left the second house in Washington, she was starting over at an age when some people are planning for retirement.

"I thought, 'Oh my God, I'm in my fifties and I'm dealing with this?'" Joyce said. "I didn't know if I could make it, but I did. We're always stronger than what we think."

Joyce's story shows that addiction can trap anyone at any time—and it doesn't have to rise to the level of opioid or heroin use to have disastrous consequences. I met her at Faith Forward in Latrobe, where she works, more than two years into her recovery. She doesn't make much at the job she got through a Westmoreland County Community College CareerLinks program that helps seniors with employment. But it supplements her disability stipends for a back problem and provides her with another recovery support system.

Her new life beats living out of a car, something she did before attempting suicide.

"I don't know how it got so bad," Joyce said. "It just snowballed and I couldn't stop. Your brain keeps telling you, 'You need more, you need more, you need more' until you've taken so many that you just die or hope you die."

Joyce, a slender, well-spoken woman, doesn't check many of the boxes that are linked to addiction, particularly when it pertains to childhood trauma. She grew up in a loving house and her father served as a Westmoreland County judge for more than three decades. Addiction was never an issue in their family. And Joyce only started taking Xanax in her thirties after it was prescribed to help with the panic attacks that she said were a result of a failed marriage.

Joyce took Xanax responsibly for years and only started abusing it after a neighbor assaulted her. She said the attack likely triggered trauma from her marriage, and her life quickly spiraled out of control. Joyce got evicted from her apartment in New Stanton and drove her family away, as it struggled to make sense of her addiction.

The day I met with Joyce, she'd just learned that one of the women who was in her recovery house died from a heroin overdose. It was a chilling warning that she can never let her guard down. Joyce's mother and daughter are also reminders to stay clean. The Greensburg resident talks to both almost every day and has repaired other family relationships that her addiction nearly destroyed. Just like her sobriety, she does not take those for granted.

"I didn't think I was going to get my family back," Joyce said. "Some people never do and it's sad."

THE
COMPLEXITY
OF RELIGION

6

A MAN WALKS INTO A CHURCH

He hadn't quite made it to his thirty-fifth birthday—and that was probably longer than he should have lived—when he reached a breaking point. Drugs had cost him everything: his wife, his kids, even a roof over his head. Strung out on heroin and cocaine and living out of his truck, he stuck a 9mm pistol in the front of his pants and headed toward a bank in Uniontown. The plan wasn't to rob it, so he could buy more drugs. The plan was to force police to shoot him, so he didn't have to turn the gun on himself.

Walking past a Catholic church, Rick Hennessey stopped when a priest asked if he could talk to him. The priest looked past the fact that a six foot, four inch, well-built man had a gun bulging out of his pants. He saw a completely lost soul, and the mercy he showed may have saved Rick's life. Once inside the church, he told the priest everything, including how he planned to end his life. Rick eventually turned his gun over to the priest, who drove him to a drug-and-alcohol rehabilitation center for his seventh attempt to get clean. Something worked this time, and Rick finally cast aside addiction and the demons that had been chasing him.

Rick is Dawn Hennessey's husband. He helped her build Faith Forward and Angel Arms, two nonprofit organizations that help people who may be as lost as he was when he came close to ending his life. He has been clean for more than fifteen years and is yet another example of why no addict is too far gone to reach.

Rick's story starts in Fayette County with an abusive father and chaotic home life, both of which forced him to grow up way too fast. It continued in Colorado where he moved after high school. He got married and worked for his father-in-law, who was building a baseball stadium in Denver for the expansion Colorado Rockies. The financing was in place, and they were about to break ground when his father-in-law died of a massive heart attack.

The tragedy sent Rick reeling, and his past behavior resurfaced. He wrote unauthorized checks totaling $30,000 to himself from a stadium fund while on a drug binge. He served three years in a state prison for felony theft. His heroin addiction almost cost him more than the bad checks did after he got out of jail.

Once, a woman passing by his apartment noticed his door was open. She saw his ankle sticking out of a room and called an ambulance after finding him overdosed in the bathroom. That call saved his life.

But his addiction continued after Rick moved back to Western Pennsylvania, and it admittedly turned him into an "animal." It got so bad that drug dealers offered to take him to rehab, so he would stop robbing them. He tried treatment facilities to make his mother happy, not the drug dealers, and to try to save his marriage. He never intended to get clean and used the time to take a break from the streets.

His marriage eventually collapsed, and he also lost his kids. Rick stopped wanting to live and might not have without meeting that priest. What really saved him after getting clean at a treatment center was turning to God and embracing religion. It led him away from Uniontown and to the church where he met Dawn. The two married after a long friendship and courtship. They later took in Isaac, the NAS baby who weighed just three pounds at birth and could fit in the palm of Rick's hand.

Rick drives across the country as a mover for Allied Vans and owns his truck. It's a measure of how secure he is in sobriety that Rick can spend weeks on the road where he could use without anyone knowing.

But he is also respectful enough of his recovery to stay away from certain TV shows or songs, lest they trigger something that make him want to use. He is also adamant about not taking opiates for pain relief. He refused them after having three teeth pulled and after cracking his elbow following a five-foot fall from his truck.

"I just can't do it because I like the feeling too much," Rick said.

He liked the feeling when he was in addiction because it numbed pain he felt from a strained and combative relationship with his father and a bad home life.

"Most addicts don't get high because that's just what they want to do," Rick said. "They get high because they're hurting; they're broken. You talk to drug addicts and something happened to them in the past that just haunts them. Most of them have ghosts."

Those ghosts still chase Rick from time to time. Three weeks before we met, his best friend was found with a needle in his chest. Not long before that, his brother-in-law also died from a heroin overdose.

Dawn and Rick Hennessey at a Project
Stand rally.

Rick has a scar on his left wrist that looks like a small horseshoe from a bar fight years ago. It is not the only reminder of the rough-and-tumble days of his youth. He was also shot three times in the shoulder during a drug deal gone bad, and Rick once needed a blood transfusion after getting stabbed.

All of it is still a relatively small price to pay for his past. Rick continues to put it in his rearview mirror through his work with Faith Forward and Angel Arms. His recovery started with an act of kindness by a priest who saw his desperation and overlooked the gun in his pants. It has continued with his surrendering to an even higher power than the priest he encountered when he was as lost as a person could be.

A born-again Christian, Rick said, "I replaced drugs with God, with religion. It may not work for everybody, but it does for me. It gives me something to believe in."

BRIDGING THE DIVIDE

Religion or spirituality plays a vital role for many addicts in recovery. In a 2017 study by Dr. Eric Kocian and Dr. John Lewis, 95 percent of the 158 addicts they interviewed at the Westmoreland County Prison said that talking to a religious leader or embracing some form of spirituality was at least somewhat helpful when trying to get clean.

Narcotics Anonymous and Alcoholics Anonymous are anchored in the idea of surrendering to a higher power. One of the more fascinating perspectives I heard about the role of religion and spirituality in the context of the opioid epidemic came from Dave Lettrich. The Latrobe resident is a preacher at Hot Metal Bridge Church on the South Side of Pittsburgh, and he ministers to addicts living in the streets.

"One of the things I love about heroin addicts is that in many ways, they understand what our relationship with God is supposed to be like better than anyone else," Lettrich said. "They love their God, heroin, with all their heart, soul, and mind. Everything else comes second. While it's misplaced, they have a better understanding of what our relationship with God is meant to be. When those people find a way to step back from that addiction and turn that same commitment and devotion toward God, it tends to be very effective."

It was with Nate Keisel. The Jeannette resident replaced his addiction with his devotion to God and Jesus Christ, although it took him awhile to get there.

Nate's addiction started in his late teens. It consumed him even after he got a break for felony theft at the age of twenty-one and landed in drug court. He relapsed time and time again, and nothing worked—not medical-assisted treatment, not rehabilitation facilities, and not halfway houses. He finally burned through so many chances in drug court that the Erie County judge who offered him leniency gave up on him.

Nate spent two years in jail, and less than a week from his release date, he reached out to the prison minister. He was desperate and knew he fell into the category that some of the corrections officers referred to as the "walking dead." These are heroin addicts at serious risk of fatally overdosing after they get out of jail because their tolerance is lower. That was Nate, and he all but begged the minister to save his life. That started the process of getting Nate into Teen Challenge, a faith-based treatment center in Cheswick. While he waited for a bed, Nate stayed at a homeless shelter.

Every Sunday, the minister picked him up for church and then took him to his house for lunch. One time, as Nate played a board game with the minister and his wife's four-year-old daughter, something struck him. His own family, aside from an aunt and uncle, never visited him in prison. Here, two people who barely knew him showed enough faith and trust in Nate to leave him alone in the living room with their daughter.

The family never treated him like a felon. The humanity and grace they displayed primed the transformation Nate eventually made at Teen Challenge. Steve Schumaker, a preacher Nate met at Teen Challenge, accelerated that process. The straight-talking Schumaker dismissed the different diagnoses Nate had received. He told him point blank that he didn't have a disease.

He said Nate wasn't an addict because of a chemical imbalance in his brain or because of a bad childhood. Schumaker told Nate that he was born selfish and enslaved to sin as a son of Adam. He put the onus on Nate to achieve freedom from it. Nate recoiled from such bluntness until one day he kicked a chair, shook his fist at God, and yelled, "What do You want from me?" He surrendered to Jesus Christ in that room and never looked back.

He completed the Teen Challenge long-term program, interned there, and later became a pastor. He earned his master's degree in theology and started the Community Mosaic Church in Jeannette. Prior to that, Nate worked as an assistant pastor at a Murrysville church, where he made a unique pairing with the pastor, an ex-police officer from Baltimore. The pastor was an ex-police officer from Baltimore. Right away, each could tell by their mannerisms that one had been a cop and one had been a convict in a former life.

"One time, he locked his keys in his office, and I said, 'I can get in there,'" Nate said with a laugh.

Nate had been clean for more than ten years when we met. He said Schumaker both simplified his issues and held him accountable for his destructive behavior. Ultimately, Nate credits the personal relationship he built with God to saving him from a life of addiction, one that he is sure would have ended from an overdose. That is the message he preaches to addicts: There is a way out, and God can show the way.

If only it was that simple.

The religious community in Westmoreland County is probably like a lot of their ilk in areas hit hard by the opioid epidemic. It wants to help and feels it has a responsibility to be part of the solution but is still trying to find its way. That is the case with Rev. Eileen Smith of Mt. Zion Church in West Newton. Smith helped start Dominion Addiction, which looks at the opioid epidemic from every angle while incorporating prayer into its services.

Smith, who worked as a nurse and state health consultant for more than two decades before joining the ministry, said the issue, "is worse than any pandemic I've seen in my public health career. Everyone needs to get involved, especially the faith-based entities because what the government is doing isn't working. The only alternative is to turn to Jesus Christ, and we need to take the lead on this."

Despite this conviction Smith is open to any solutions to the opioid epidemic, a pragmatism that reflects her past in nursing. The frustration she deals with in trying to help was evident at a Dominion Addiction service I attended. It drew a handful of people and no leaders from other churches in the West Newton area. Mt. Zion is a small, African-American church in a predominately white area, and Smith is critical of the lack of support it receives. Churches, she said, need to transcend denomination, race, and anything else that differentiates them and focus on what unites them.

Nate believes churches need to do a better job of embracing those battling addiction and working with those in the recovery community who don't have strong religious convictions.

"Unfortunately, a lot of times, the church has fallen into that self-righteous frame of mind, and so the secular community has an aversion to religion," Nate said. "The church has done a bad job of reflecting who Jesus was. He spent time with the sinners, the broken, and came out against religious leaders who were self-righteous and judgmental. If we could better communicate in Christianity who Jesus was, maybe that aversion wouldn't be there."

Nate is the type who can bridge these differences because of where he once was—and where he is now.

"The struggles today aren't, 'Where am I going to get my next fix? How am I going to steal? Am I going to die today?'" he said. "Now, it's 'How do I love my family when I'm so dang busy?' Still serious struggles to me but different. It's crazy."

A PRACTICAL SOLUTION

Dawn Hennessey has worked in addiction for more than twenty years. Yet, it still perplexes her, especially when she looks at it through the prism of the opioid epidemic.

"Imagine a little pill or substance that can totally destroy your life," she said. "It's hard to wrap your mind around how something can take over your entire life. I feel like part of what we're doing is trying to make sense of it instead of trying to fix it. And I don't think we'll ever make sense of it. You can't even find a common thread with addiction."

Dawn is convinced that faith is part of the solution as evidenced by the names of her non-profit organizations, Faith Forward and Angel Arms. What frustrates her is that the religious community in Westmoreland County has not been able to harness what could be a powerful resource against the opioid epidemic. There has been a lot of prayer, but that hasn't translated into the united front that could be a real force.

Shortly after talking to Dawn about what the religious community can do, I met two people who have fused prayer and action. If I had any doubts how much his religion drives Gus DiRenna, they evaporated after he pulled me into a prayer circle in the Carrick section of Pittsburgh.

We were chatting at a house that Gus and Rev. Jay Geisler were fixing up to turn into a recovery home, less than two miles from where Gus almost died after overdosing behind a gas station. Gus led five of us in a serenity prayer and continued: "God, thank You for bringing this crew from all different walks of life to spread good vibrations into this house. We know that You're working in many ways, God, that we can't see. Help us remember that when we go forward to do our tasks, realizing it adds up."

It was fitting that Gus and Jay held hands during the prayer. The two joined them figuratively almost ten years earlier and have since promoted long-term recovery by providing affordable housing, jobs, job-training, and support for those battling addiction. That Gus is a Methodist and Jay is an Episcopalian priest is inconsequential to them.

"What's your (religious) dogma?" Gus asked. "Let's not get into that. How about this? Do you believe addicts should get fair housing and job opportunities? Yes. Well, let's work on what we both believe in."

Despite coming from different religious denominations, Gus and Jay have built a recovery model that any faith-based organization can copy.

Take the house where Gus led us in prayer.

Jay bought it for a little less than $15,000, which included closing costs. Gus planned to put another $15,000 into it to pay for renovations plus another $15,000 to pay people in other recovery houses to help fix it up.

The house, when finished, will have five bedrooms, two bathrooms, a large kitchen, and a community area. Rent will range from $400 to $500, with each resident having his own room and job opportunities through Gus to pay rent. A manager will live in the house and run everything. The man they chose for this house has been in recovery for four years and will one day be given the option of owning the home, even with bad credit stemming from his years in addiction.

After a couple of years, Gus and Jay will offer the man the house under terms much more favorable than most people receive from a bank or mortgage company. The man, if he buys it, will have the option of keeping it as a recovery house or converting it into apartments.

The goal is to turn a former addict into a homeowner and take proceeds from the sale to start another recovery home. Repeat this process enough times, and it adds up to something significant in the battle against the opioid epidemic.

Gus DiRenna at a Carrick house that he helped turn into a recovery home.

"We're beginning with the end in mind," said Jay, head of St. Peter's Episcopal Church in the Brentwood section of Pittsburgh. "We want a productive, responsible member of society, and there's lots of ways to do it. Look, if there's a national epidemic, let's mobilize the forces and not from the top but from the grassroots."

He said churches are positioned to lead the way because many have resources, including property, and a desire to help. Churches aren't motivated by profit, Jay said, but would benefit from a small but steady revenue stream that recovery houses provide. The big payoff would come in a practical solution to the opioid epidemic that transcends prayer.

Such big-picture thinking, with religion at the foundation, binds Gus and Jay and makes them an effective duo. They want it to spread because they believe it can make a difference.

"The one player who has something to offer has been sitting on the sidelines, and that's the church," Gus said. "They're the people that we need because they have a lot of love, and they believe in prayer. They own buildings and have money. They're not in it to make a profit. They just want to help the community and build their churches back up again. They're the key to turning this around."

A HIGHER POWER

Katrin Schall is as comfortable sponsoring addicts who are atheists as she is standing with those who sing and sway and shout their love for Jesus. The Youngstown resident moves seamlessly among the different recovery sectors—religious and secular, medical-assisted treatment and total abstinence—so it made perfect sense where I first met her. It was at Mt. Zion Church before one of the services that are part of its Dominion Addiction program. The two-hour service featured addiction testimony and a fire-and-brimstone service. The underlying message was surrendering to Jesus, something that Kat attributes to her long-term sobriety.

A certified recovery specialist, Kat wasn't there to talk about Jesus but rather methadone, the narcotic that weans addicts off heroin and is flatly rejected by some in the religious community. She tried it during one of her many attempts to get clean but placed the blame for it not working on herself.

"My motives were not pure," she said.

She did not advocate for or denounce methadone that night at Mt. Zion Church. Her goal was to educate people since her guiding philosophy to recovery is whatever it takes. Kat's past is a big reason why she doesn't judge when helping addicts.

She grew up in turmoil that included an alcoholic father who once knocked out her mother with a dining room chair and threw knives and beer cans at Kat and her older brothers. The family moved often because her father gambled away rent money.

Her mom finally left her dad when Kat was thirteen, but she worked full-time, and Kat fell into the wrong crowd. She started drinking and smoking marijuana in her teens and later experimented with cocaine and LSD. She dropped out of Latrobe High School after getting pregnant and had the first of her two daughters at eighteen. She moved in with her daughter's father and resumed partying. She used and sold cocaine and was introduced to heroin by her best friend.

"I remember the day I tried it because I told myself I'd never do that," Kat said. "I had been eating pills because pills aren't scary. There's no needles. The first time I did heroin, I snorted it; I didn't shoot it. It was only a tiny bit, so it was kind of like, 'What the hell, I'll try it.' That was the next eleven years of my life."

Those next eleven years were hell on earth.

Kat managed stretches where she steered clear of heroin but still drank. A bad break-up led her back to heroin, and even the death of her best friend didn't stop her. That happened after her friend overdosed after she was raped, robbed, and left for dead. She stayed on life support for three months before the plug was pulled. She was buried on her twenty-seventh birthday.

Kat overdosed six weeks later. A friend saved her with CPR, but he'd pounded on her chest so hard that it left her with bruises. Kat responded to the near-death experience by going home and shooting more heroin.

"That's how insane (addiction) is," she said. "That was the beginning of the worst run."

She stopped caring about what happened to her, and it got worse after a family tragedy. While Kat was in prison for a drug-related offense, one of her brothers died in a car accident. When she got out, she went on a three-week drug binge. She became pregnant again and, after another prison stint, married her second daughter's father. They blended their family of four kids.

"We were like the most dysfunctional Brady Bunch in the world," Kat said.

Still, she worked and went back to school. She also completed her parole and probation requirements. She was on a better path until her world came crashing down when, she said, her stepson molested her older daughter. The pain and guilt from that overwhelmed Kat, and she went to her default for numbing the pain. That started her on her final drug "run," which covered two years and five felony convictions.

It ended when state police officers kicked in the front door and raided her house. One of the arresting officers had investigated her daughter's molestation, and Kat will never forget the sheer look of disgust on his face when he busted her.

"I knew I was going down and it just was whether it was in a body bag or handcuffs, and I didn't care either way," Kat said. "That's the point (where) I was."

She didn't feel much better even after she got a break from a lengthy prison sentence. Her public defender asked if she'd ever received treatment. Kat told him she had always gone to jail after her drug-related arrests. She was looking at a sentence of two to five years for crimes that included dealing but served four months with the stipulation that she complete intensive outpatient treatment.

Treatment lasted six hours a day on weekdays, and she couldn't drink because her ankle bracelet detected alcohol. Confined to house arrest, Kat was drug tested often and only allowed supervised visits with her kids.

"I hated my existence," she said. "I hated every single day of my life."

It got worse. One of her counselors told her she had to start attending 12-step meetings. Kat told her to kiss off. How much more could she possibly learn about her messed up life? However, given the option of prison or meetings, she chose the latter. She still had no intention of pursuing long-term recovery. She went to church one day, but it was to tell God how angry she was at Him for taking her brother and father.

Kris Langdon, the pastor that day, talked about a loving and forgiving God and made an impression on Kat. She connected with Langdon and his wife, Robyn, joined their church, and eventually turned her life over to Jesus. Kat also embraced the 12-step approach after she came to a sick realization about her sponsor. Kat had once dealt drugs to the woman's sister, who later disappeared and remains missing to this day. The woman knew exactly who Kat was and yet still helped her.

"She sat across the table, working with me to try to save my life," Kat said. "It made me believe in this so-called fellowship."

The inclusiveness Kat felt when she finally achieved long-term sobriety now guides her as a certified recovery specialist.

"I'm not going to exclude somebody because they're not going to believe or pray to the same God that I believe in," Kat said. "I sponsor women who are just as on fire for Jesus as I am. But I (also) sponsor women who don't want to go to church. It's tricky."

She tries to simplify it by stressing how elastic the definition of a higher power is. It might come in the form of someone at church proclaiming their love for Jesus as tears stream down their face. It might be someone who doesn't want to die from an overdose because their parents will never be the same. It might be someone who doesn't want to use because it will break their grandmother's heart.

"Even two addicts talking is a power bigger than themselves," Kat said. "Someone talking to me before they make a decision is a power greater than yourself. It doesn't have to be a deity."

If religion is the path to recovery, even that is fraught with complexity. Those who firmly believe that Jesus is the only way to achieve long-term sobriety risk excluding or alienating addicts from other religions. They may even give pause to those who believe in God and Jesus but not enough to become a born-again Christian.

The latter approach would have pushed Kat away had it been a hard sell.

"If Pastor Kris had said, 'You have to accept Jesus Christ today or you're going to die' it would have never worked," Kat said. "I had to come to those terms on my own. He and Robyn just loved me until I got there. They didn't judge me because of the things I had done or where I had been. That's where the faith-based community is struggling in trying to address this because they want to put a deity on (recovery), and it's pushing people away."

Katrin Schall speaking at Mt. Zion Church in West Newton.

Like Nate Keisel, Kat is well-positioned to connect the religious and secular communities.

Ask her why she has been able to maintain her sobriety for more than seven years, and she will say Jesus.

"Period. End of story."

But she also knows from her own experience and what she sees in her job that it would be fruitless if not dangerous to insist that what worked for her will work for other addicts. If someone needs methadone or Suboxone to stay clean, Kat has no problem with that. She also supports shooting galleries for addicts and needle exchanges to help keep addicts alive, so they one day have a chance at recovery. To Kat, it's not how addicts achieve long-term recovery. What matters is that they get there.

"There's not a one-size-fits-all answer," she said.

Kat is a textbook example of that and she tried several approaches before one finally worked for her. Her life has been completely different since getting clean in 2011.

A high school dropout who got her GED in prison, Kat earned a bachelor's degree in psychology with a specialization in addiction. Once a sixty-bag a day heroin user, she is working toward a master's degree. Kat is on the Westmoreland County drug court and helped develop a program for the county prison where she counsels addicts.

"The biggest thing I say is education is power," Kat said. "Do research. Find out for yourself what may be best for you."

Even if isn't religion, that doesn't exclude reliance on a higher power in recovery.

"Purpose is the biggest thing that's missing when someone is trying to find recovery," Kat said. "Most of the dreams addicts had can't become reality because of what they've done, because of the bridges that they have burned. So now they have to find their purpose. That's spirituality in itself."

THE WAY TO SALVATION

Her addict mind thought that she might get some free heroin from the man as thanks for taking him to her dealer, not the danger of getting into a van with a stranger. The man who asked Elba Ramos where he could buy heroin raped her at gunpoint in the back of the van. She is lucky he didn't leave her for dead.

Three months pregnant at the time of the attack, she spiraled deeper into heroin abuse. Using numbed the lingering psychological pain but couldn't quiet the voice in her head. The one that told her she couldn't possibly have this baby because it would be a daily reminder of the rape.

Six months into a tortured pregnancy, she went to an abortion clinic. Nurses pleaded with her not to do it since her baby had a heartbeat. But she insisted on aborting the pregnancy and received an injection that induced labor. She gave birth to a stillborn son.

The nurses knew she was an addict; they placed her baby next to her so she could see what she had done. She had always wanted a son, and when she looked at him, it struck her how much he looked like his father. She stroked his eyebrows before screaming, "Take him away! Take him away!"

Elba spent the next six months on the same diabolical treadmill. She killed the pain with drugs, but the more she used, the worse she felt. She covered the mirrors in her house because she couldn't bear to look at herself in any of them. One day she reached her breaking point. She was married with three daughters, none older than seven, but she couldn't bring herself to want to live for them. She cried out to God, beseeching Him to save her life—if He was real.

Almost three decades later, I encountered Elba crying out to God for a different reason. She was leading a Friday night service at Father's Heart Church with Pastor Henry Taliercio. Listening to her, it became obvious that the microphone she held served as a prop more than anything. She certainly had no need for it as she boomed out her love for Jesus and encouraged others to also let loose.

Pastor Elba is the embodiment of Father's Heart, which occupies close to an entire block in a quiet section of Jeannette, if not the soul of it. She is passionate, a little in your face and convinced that God and Jesus are *the* way out of the opioid epidemic. Or at least the way out of the personal hell of addiction.

There is an absolutism that pervades Father's Heart, and that is precisely the point. The church and its two in-patient rehabilitation facilities (one for women is in Jeannette, and one for men is in McKeesport) refuses government money because it never wants to compromise its mission. That's why it survives solely on donations that don't come with stipulations.

"I'd rather put a padlock on the door than (accept grants) because if we can't bring Jesus in, I don't want to be in it," Henry said.

Henry is a somewhat unlikely head of Father's Heart. The Brooklyn native ran with the Mafia back in the 1970s and became addicted to heroin while also spreading it in New York City. He tried traditional rehabilitation treatment facilities, but nothing worked until he ended up in a faith-based center and turned his life over to God.

Henry started an outreach center in Brooklyn that fed the homeless and ministered to those battling drug and alcohol addiction. The seeds of his relocation to rural Westmoreland County were planted during a meeting with the pastor of Word of Life Ministries in Hempfield Township while on a national fundraising tour. The pastor asked him to join his church. Henry said, "Are you crazy? Leave New York and come here?"

After praying about it for two years, he made the move. He stayed at Word of Life for five years before leaving a job with a comfortable salary to start Father's Heart where money is scarce.

"We just make it," he said. "But we're making it, so that in itself is a miracle."

Henry is confined to a wheelchair because of a rare muscle disease, but he has a commanding presence at Father's Heart—whether he is leading a Friday night service or eating lunch with the women who live in the treatment facility. He looks like Al Pacino and has the same deep, scratchy voice as the iconic actor. Like Elba, he is unwavering in his devotion to God and his belief that He is the way to life after addiction.

A typical day at Father's Heart includes praise and worship in the morning, Bible study and counseling throughout the day, and worship at night. The Bible is the foundation of its recovery paradigm, but Henry said counseling is also critical to getting to the root cause of addiction.

Pastor Elba Ramos speaking at Father's Heart Church in Jeannette.

"If I lock you in the basement for a week, you no longer have a drug problem because once the addiction is kicked, there's not a drug problem," he said. "But there's still a heart and brain problem. There's a lot of insecurities that cause people to do drugs. Unless you get to those issues, they'll never stop using drugs. Counseling is critical because even if they go through a program, it won't matter if we don't get to the root issues of their issues."

Bona Ferluckaj is one of Father's Heart success stories. She'd been on the staff for a year and half when we met. Bona's perpetual smile says everything about how far she has come after getting hooked on prescription medication and eventually heroin.

"I wanted to die every day when I was addicted to heroin," said Bona, who is originally from Staten Island, New York. "Every day, I woke up just praying I would die."

She almost did with her brother. The two overdosed while using together. The paramedic who saved them told them they were minutes away from dying. A month later, Bona met two pastors in Brooklyn who set her up with Pastor Henry and put her on a train. She laughs when she looks back at what she thought when she left bustling New York City for the rolling hills of Western Pennsylvania.

"I was like, Oh my God, where am I? Where's the people? Is this real?" she recalled.

Her perspective has changed since finding herself at Father's Heart and graduating from its program in 2014.

"They've become my family," Bona said. "It's so surreal that sometimes it doesn't feel real. That's the love of Christ that flows through them."

Bona is of Albanian descent and was raised a Muslim. She converted to Christianity at Father's Heart, even though it caused a strain with some family members, and hasn't looked back. She works with the women in the program and prays with them. Arguably her biggest contribution is simply her presence since she is an example that recovery is possible from addiction.

Mark Vega is one, too. He had been at Father's Heart in McKeesport for almost a year when we met before a Friday night service at the Jeannette church.

Mark, fifty-one years old, was a month away from graduating from the men's program, and as we chatted, he told me about a life of tragedy. It included losing his best friend to a freak baseball accident and his father to cancer. Mark joined a gang at the age of sixteen and said he spent decades as an "enforcer" in it. He sold and used drugs, and his heroin addiction eventually cost him everything. Just one year earlier, he was living in a homeless shelter in Brooklyn but found his way to Father's Heart. He had renounced the violence and hedonism that defined his earlier life and reestablished relationships with his two sons.

"The man you see here," he said pointing to himself, "is not the man that used to be."

That is the message I got from Elba when I met with her a couple of days later. Clean for twenty-eight years, she inspired her husband to do the same. They turned their life over to God and built a different life for their family. Elba became an ordained minister in 2008 and later helped Henry start Father's Heart. Like Henry, she rejects medical-assisted treatment as a way to sobriety. She sees methadone and Suboxone not as legitimate recovery tools but as swapping one addiction for another.

"Methadone is legalized heroin," Elba said. "Did God create you to be on a chemical for the rest of your life? What changes people is God and your faith that there has to be something greater that can change who you are."

Elba is not shy about sharing her convictions, as rigid as they may come across.

"People look at us (like), 'Oh, they're such religious freaks,'" she said. "I'm not here to sell God. I'm here to tell you that I lived that life, and my life is not the same (because of God). And that's what I give these girls."

SLOWING DOWN LIFE

The mother of a twenty-year-old man approached Bishop Edward Malesic and asked him to baptize her son. Malesic found the request a little odd and wondered if the young man had a terminal disease. No, the mother told him, he is an addict, and she'd found him three times after he overdosed.

Encounters like that are what spurred the leader of the Roman Catholic Diocese of Greensburg to act. In 2017, he formed a task force with the mandate to confront the opioid epidemic with prayer and awareness. Seven prayer sessions drew a total of 1,000 people—and confirmed to Malesic what he had heard prior to forming the task force.

"I am out in the public quite a bit with confirmations, wedding anniversaries, and celebrations, and invariably someone will come up and ask me to pray for their son. Sometimes it's a typical thing like he needs a job, he's struggling with a marriage," Malesic said. "But now a lot of times it's 'He's on drugs. I don't know what to do.' I also began to hear from my priests, 'Bishop, we need to do something. I buried somebody this week who died of an overdose.' I do believe in the power of prayer. I've seen it work miracles. So, we have to keep praying, but then prayer has to lead to some sort of action."

What resonated with me most after chatting with Malesic is that when he talked about the societal need to reclaim Sunday, he wasn't just talking about the religious aspect of it.

"I know people don't believe me when I say this, but when we gave Sundays away as a family day, as a day of God, we lost a lot," Malesic said. "I went to church, against my will, then we had to visit my grandfather, and then we came home and had a big meal. Then we lounged around and went for a drive. We don't do that anymore."

Indeed, lazy days once reserved for recharging and reflecting are part of a bygone era, bulky eight-track tapes in an age of sleek, high-definition TVs. They have been usurped by days that don't end so much as they run together because they are cranked up to the highest speed.

To Dr. Eric Kocian, there is a cause and effect to the sensory overload that has become routine.

"There are more people that are suffering from depression and addiction. I wonder if it's that norms are changing, and we really haven't been taking that time to set aside for ourselves and just chill out," said Kocian, a St. Vincent College criminology professor who has studied addiction in Westmoreland County. "We're constantly on the go, and our bodies weren't made to be under a constant state of fight or flight. It doesn't work like that. Put the phone down, turn the music off, mediate, pray, let your brain settle."

The great paradox is that with the Internet and proliferation of mobile devices, we are more connected than ever but also just as disconnected. Go to a restaurant or a coffee shop, and it is not uncommon to see two people sitting at the same table but not talking. They are on their phones, maybe checking news on one of the echo chambers that make politics more divisive than ever. They might even be texting one another while sitting a couple of feet apart. This is the new American way of communicating.

Nothing more typifies how we talk to each other without really connecting than social media.

"I honestly believe that, as a society, we are training ourselves to be worse listeners because of all of the social media stuff that we engage in," Kocian said. "If you think about Twitter or Facebook, all you're doing is sending out your thoughts and you're not really listening; there's no dialogue or conversation. You're posting your thoughts, your opinions, your beliefs. In the process, you're not really connected with anybody."

"We always say the opposite of active addiction is connection, and how are we connecting these people?" said Tim Phillips, executive director of the Westmoreland County Drug Overdose Task Force. "Wherever they are, we need to keep them connected."

Tim was talking about people battling addiction. But human connection is also a key to preventing addiction, experts say. That is becoming more difficult as community becomes less defined. It means different things to different generations, such as James Bumar, who would scoff at the idea that internet chatrooms are genuine communities.

I met with Bumar about six months before he retired as Latrobe Chief of Police. He has never seen anything more destructive than the opioid epidemic—from the families it has torn apart to the spin-off crime it has unleashed. He wondered if things might be different if we could go back to a simpler time, such as when he grew up.

"We were at the playground in the morning, the pool in the afternoon, and the playground at night," said Bumar, a lifelong resident of the Latrobe area. "We had nothing, but we had everything. We were so entertained by simple things. You try to entertain a kid now without a screen or a keyboard, forget it."

Bumar grudgingly carries a cell phone and good luck getting him to embrace text messaging. In his early years on the police force, many of the calls they received were from residents complaining they couldn't get into their driveway because kids were playing football or hockey in the street. Neighborhood streets now aren't nearly as lively as Bumar remembered. The same is true of playgrounds, creating an undesired vacuum.

"Now you're getting calls to playgrounds because people are dealing drugs," Bumar said. "The kind of kids that should be at the playground aren't at the playground. It's a different world. I don't envy kids growing up in this day and age."

Carmen Capozzi of Sage's Army is among those battling the opioid epidemic who see a link between the instant gratification that technology has fostered and the epidemic. Add the ubiquity of medication that treats pain and regulates emotions, and the opioid epidemic, to Carmen, is a tragic reflection of how society has changed.

"Everything now is a quick fix," he said. "Years ago, you held onto your TV for ten, fifteen years. If it broke, you took it to the TV repairman. Now you just throw it away and go buy another one. How do you change a quick-fix mentality?"

Kocian said slowing things down just a little bit is helpful for anyone. It gives them time to focus on themselves and develop or strengthen coping skills. This can be done through prayer or meditation. Or, it can be as simple turning off the TV and putting the phone down for a small portion of the day.

Malesic said one simple thing that could pay huge dividends is for families to sit down together for a meal. No phones. No TVs. Just real conversation.

"It's not rocket science," he said. "We simply don't have personal connections the way we once did, which goes against our human nature to be social."

What results is a void that allows addiction to thrive.

"The problem with addiction isn't the drug because there will always be drugs," said Dr. Paul Niemiec, the director of counseling services for the Roman Catholic Diocese of Greensburg. "The issue is the lack of connection, the lack of meaning, the inability to feel part of a family, a community, spirituality. People don't have that."

Malesic said religion is a way of preventing drug and alcohol abuse and helping someone in recovery because of the foundation it provides.

"People need to talk about a basic element of their human lives, which is their soul," Malesic said. "We don't talk about it, we don't foster it, and we don't say you need to nourish it. Those who finally have a chance to talk to someone about who they are and hear that they're loved and that there is a God who wants them to become whole, it makes a difference because it is true. There is a sense of community within a church. It's a place where you look out for one another."

THERE
IS
HOPE

LOST AND FOUND

Lost Dreams Awakening, an oasis amidst the opioid epidemic, has the initial feel of a warehouse.

It is large enough that a refrigerator and stove tucked in one corner can almost hide in plain sight. At the other end of the cavernous space is a living room complete with easy chairs, a couch and a large TV mounted to a wall. For Kyle Sundo's family, it is more than just a place to relax.

There are framed pictures of Kyle on the wall. In between them hangs what looks like an oversized penny with a silhouette of a boy and a dog etched onto the copper plate. Kyle loved dogs, so it's a fitting sign for the area of Lost Dreams Awakening dubbed "Kyle's Korner." Kyle loved people, too, something that didn't change even as his addiction to pain pills, and later heroin, consumed him.

"He was the most likable kid you could ever want to meet and just a ball of fun," said Barb Penn, Kyle's aunt. "He was very respectful and never left without kissing people goodbye."

Kyle died of a heroin overdose in 2016 and was buried on his twenty-second birthday. His family and Lost Dreams Awakening make sure he isn't just a number. Kyle's death inspired the "warm handoff" program that Lost Dreams Awakening runs in conjunction with several Allegheny County hospitals. The program engages people who overdosed and tries to get them into treatment straight from the hospital. The approach aims to eliminate the gap that may have claimed Kyle's life. He was living with Barb and his grandmother when he overdosed and was taken to Allegheny General Hospital.

He told Barb that he wanted to die so he could be with his grandfather. She tried to get him placed in a psych ward. But Kyle denied saying anything suicidal, and the hospital had no choice but to release him. Two mornings later was found in bed with a needle in his arm.

Barb honors his memory by running the warm hand-off program and speaking out against stigma. She is well-positioned to do both. Barb is a board member at Lost Dreams Awakening, where Kyle's parents also volunteer. She is also a long-time secretary in the Allegheny General Hospital emergency room and isn't shy about voicing her disgust over the attitude she sees toward patients who overdose.

"It drives me crazy how they treat people," she said. "The stigma these kids face is just horrible."

Working with doctors and nurses to change mindsets is part of the warm hand-off program. Any time Barb needs a reminder of what she is fighting for, all she has to do is stop at Kyle's Korner.

"So many people tell me when they come sit in here they just feel this overwhelming peace," Barb said.

Lost Dreams Awakening has become a second home for Barb and not just because it keeps her close to Kyle.

There is a quaintness to Lost Dreams Awakening that belies its sheer size. Spend a couple of hours there and the room that looks large enough to double as an airport hangar seems to shrink. There is a friendly vibe to the place, as if the door to it is a pair of open arms.

That is exactly what Dr. VonZell Wade and Laurie Johnson-Wade envisioned when they started Lost Dreams Awakening in the back of a New Kensington drug-and-alcohol treatment center.

Since its 2014 opening, Lost Dreams Awakening has been at the forefront of the opioid epidemic battle. It is involved in all aspects of it, from raising awareness and placing addicts in treatment to helping addicts transition after in-patient rehabilitation stays and providing support to family members affected by addiction.

The essence of Lost Dreams Awakening is much more basic. Anyone who walks in is welcome, whether they simply want to grab a cup of coffee or they are having a really bad day and trying not to get high.

"When I look around and see these people in a safe place and they're clean, even if it's just for that day, it's well worth it," VonZell said.

So are celebrations likes the one that took place the day I visited Lost Dreams Awakening. Shortly before noon, everyone gathered around thirty-two-year-old Rachel Fox at the front of the room. Rachel stood in front of a chocolate cake, and she had playfully switched the candles from thirty-two to twenty-three.

Clean for just over a year, Rachel almost lost one of her legs after a heroin overdose. She spent a full year in leg braces and had to learn to walk again. Those braces seemed like a distant memory as she stood smiling while VonZell and Laurie led us in singing "Happy Birthday."

Laurie Johnson-Wade and Rachel Fox at Lost Dreams Awakening.

205

"If people could grasp the power that's in just one story," Laurie said. "Rachel's another year older after being on death's door many times. Something finally clicked."

The same thing happened with VonZell and Laurie almost three decades earlier.

*   *   *

VonZell is a clinical psychologist at Spirit Life, a comprehensive drug and alcohol rehabilitation facility that spreads across a couple of hundred acres near Indiana. The setting and a small grotto at the main entrance gives Spirit Life a tranquil feel. I met VonZell there a couple of months before visiting Lost Dreams Awakening and learned the hard road he'd traveled to his work with other addicts.

VonZell's path to addiction started in a house where it wasn't uncommon to see cocaine on a table. He ran with his older cousins and drank and smoked marijuana with them. That escalated to crack cocaine, and his drug use and dealing landed him in prison several times.

At one point, his mother refused to bail him out of jail, forcing VonZell to think about changing his life. He and Laurie were dating when she got clean and started faithfully attending Narcotics Anonymous meetings. VonZell tried to follow her example, but his vows to stay sober usually ended after a week or two, and he returned to the same crowd. Laurie finally told VonZell that he needed to go to an inpatient facility and commit to recovery if he wanted to have a future with her.

He relented and stayed clean for eighty-nine days before relapsing. He promptly returned to rehab and has never looked back. VonZell has been clean since August 4, 1991.

More impressive is what he did after achieving long-term sobriety. He went to Westmoreland County Community College in his mid-thirties and became a drug-and-alcohol counselor. He continued his education and graduated from Duquesne University with a PhD in psychology.

"It sort of blows my mind that I had the tenacity and perseverance to do something at a prestigious university such as Duquesne," VonZell said. "Even now, this whole doctor title freaks me out sometimes."

His doctor title is one of his most effective tools in showing people battling addiction what they can do if they stay off drugs.

"That's one of the reasons I pursued higher education," VonZell said. "To show people it can be done."

VonZell is the clinical director at Spirit Life, but if he didn't have a mortgage and other bills to pay, he would work full-time at Lost Dreams Awakening. That is how committed he is to grass-roots activism. Recovery meetings at Lost Dreams Awakening reflect the inclusive approach that VonZell and Laurie take when working with addicts. Some people in the meetings are on medical-assisted treatment such as methadone and Suboxone. Others are strict adherents of Narcotics Anonymous, which philosophically rejects medical-assisted treatment. All of the addicts come together because they are bound by a common goal.

"They want to improve their quality of life and although it isn't complete abstinence (for some), they take the time to come to a meeting and share their struggles," VonZell said. "I love being around people who look at their life and want to improve it. I think the most powerful influence I have is that I have walked in those shoes. I understand when people say they want to use."

So does Laurie. I met her for the first time when I visited Lost Dreams Awakening, and it took about five minutes to figure out that she is the fire to VonZell's ice. Laurie's force of personality served Lost Dreams Awakening well when she and VonZell dipped into their own pockets just to keep the lights on at their nonprofit organization. She is plainspoken and direct as a gut punch—whether she is criticizing a system that forces grassroots organizations to compete for grant money or telling an addict why he or she needs to get their butt into treatment.

"Here, we're boots on the ground, peer to peer," Laurie said. "The whole thing works from the bottom up."

Like VonZell, Laurie battled her own addiction, which stemmed from a lifelong struggle with her weight. She tried diets. She tried hypnosis. She finally tried cocaine. That led her down a path that ended when Laurie "got tired of being put in a cage." She was two weeks away from the twenty-seventh anniversary of her clean date when we talked, and she is every bit as committed as VonZell to her sobriety and helping others plagued by substance abuse.

Laurie is a certified behavior analyst, a certified recovery specialist, and a certified recovery coach. She develops recovery support programs at Spirit Life, and they are also a priority of hers at Lost Dreams Awakening. Helping addicts bridge the gap, before they get into a treatment program and after they leave it, is her passion. She has seen too many people fall through the cracks. She takes those deaths personally.

"That is somebody's child, and they have a name," Laurie said. "When they were a baby, nobody thought this would be their end."

There are scattered pictures on Lost Dreams Awakening's walls of people who lost their lives to overdoses. There are about fifty more pictures in storage. That doesn't make those deaths any less significant or hurtful, but VonZell and Laurie want the prevailing message of Lost Dreams Awakening to be that recovery is possible.

Spending part of a day there crystallized something VonZell told me earlier at Spirit Life. His approach to his life's work is simple: win the small battles, and they will add up to something bigger.

"Help that individual," he said. "If you can (save) one, that's one less person that's going to overdose and die. That's one less family that will have to grieve. That's one less child that will be without a parent. That's where the true perspective is."

Tony Sobotka is among the regulars at Lost Dreams Awakening, and his perspective has changed since getting involved there. He started attending family counseling sessions there with his granddaughter as she battled heroin addiction. He outlasted her at Lost Dreams Awakening (she is doing well in recovery and moved away) and is now there so often that he is simply known as "Pap." He volunteers at Lost Dreams Awakening in a number of ways, whether it is taking pictures for the fashion shows that Lost Dreams Awakening stages to raise money or by giving rides to people who don't have driving privileges.

When his granddaughter became addicted to heroin Pap thought, like many from his generation, that it was a death sentence. His views changed as he became more involved with Lost Dreams Awakening and a convenience store conversation reversed his thinking. He told a cashier he'd known for years that he was buying supplies for his granddaughter, who was in rehab. She stuck out her hand for him to shake it and said, "I'm in recovery too."

Pap choked up a little as he recounted the story.

"It opened my eyes," he said. "There's this beautiful little girl holding down a job, and she's a recovering addict. That gave me hope. She gave me a present that no one else can ever give to me."

He is paying it forward.

Pap has educated himself on addiction and is training to become a recovery coach at the age of sixty-eight. Like others, he simply loves hanging out at Lost Dreams Awakening—whether it is watching Steelers games or just chatting.

That he is Pap to most people there is just fine with him. It's what his granddaughter calls him, and it stuck. Just like he did at Lost Dreams Awakening.

"There's probably people here who don't even know my real name," he said with a chuckle.

FINDING HIS WAY

The text I received from Greg Powell that he'd just celebrated a two-year anniversary of sobriety didn't surprise me. What did was when I reconnected with Greg and learned about the makeovers that have nothing, yet everything, to do with his ongoing recovery.

The makeovers qualify as extreme since they include getting his nails painted and makeup applied to his face. But Greg, who had been shot at by drug dealers and had been in more fights than he can remember, just can't say no to his nieces.

"These two little girls have helped me more than anything else recover from my accident," said Greg, who was hit by a train in 2016. "They're my best friends, loving me and letting me be their uncle. They don't even realize it, and I don't know how to express it to them. Being around them puts a smile on my face." What isn't as simple as doting on his nieces is what comes next for him.

As much progress as Greg had made, he wasn't any farther along on the future than when we had talked almost four months earlier. He feels a pull to the ministry given the foundation that religion provides in his recovery. But beyond that, it is hard for Greg to see many other opportunities as he puts his life back together.

He worked in construction for more than a decade and was offered a job as a foreman before his accident. But returning to what he knows best is not an option due to lingering balance issues and the reality that a workplace injury could kill him if he gets hit in the head.

Also working against him is a police record with felonies on it and no driver's license.

"I'm thirty-five years old, live at home and have nothing going on," Greg said. "I had some things going on in my life, and I lost them through poor decisions."

The struggle to find his way is common for people in long-term recovery.

"I don't ever have cravings but sometimes I wonder who I am and what the hell I'm doing," he said. "Sometimes the thought of falling back into the comfortable place I know too well creeps in. I understand the life of stealing, lying, manipulating, going to prison, getting out, getting high. Sometimes it gets hard to keep grounded and balanced."

The connections he has reestablished since getting clean help Greg, and those go beyond his family.

A couple of days before Christmas 2017, he told his story to a group of students at West Mifflin High School. Afterward a girl approached him and told Greg that he'd been friends with her mom and dad. The two started chatting, and it quickly dawned on Greg that he was talking to the girl who lost her father before she was even born.

He flashed back to that fateful night more than a decade earlier when Greg was at a party and a fight broke out. Greg's friend got hit so hard that he died from blunt-force trauma to the head. Greg eventually lost touch with the girl's mother, but she reached out to him after his talk at West Mifflin. He now spends time with the girl and her mother. They have gone bowling, and he even joined them for pedicures.

"I get to see my friend's daughter growing up," he said. "I never thought that would happen. She does well in school, doesn't drink, doesn't do drugs. She's very grown up."

The same is true of Greg even if he sometimes struggles to see it as he looks at an uncertain future. The difference now, however, is that he has the mechanisms to cope with problems and a strong support system anchored by his family and church. Greg once saw drugs as the answer to his problems. Now he sees them as the cause of the problems that ultimately stemmed from his addiction.

"I am proud of myself for how far I've come," Greg said. "I think about what I've put my family through. I think about the people who depend on me. One poor decision doesn't back me up one day. It backs me up two and a half years."

It is a miracle that he has lived beyond that fateful walk on the railroad tracks. Greg was in such dire shape when first responders got to him that he had no vital signs. They used electric paddles to bring him back to life. Even after they rushed him to the hospital, they weren't sure he would survive.

Greg is still dealing with fallout from the accident. He has breathing issues, and more surgeries loom. Doctors aren't sure he will ever recover his sense of smell. In addition, a bright light or a loud noise can trigger post-traumatic stress disorder (PTSD) and send him into a fit of anger. Even with all of the complications, Greg knows he is lucky he didn't suffer what would have been a tragic symmetry.

The accident occurred three days before his thirty-third birthday. He was taken to Forbes Hospital in Monroeville—where his mother had given birth to him.

"What if I had died on the same day in the same hospital where I was born?" he said. "It's crazy."

As Greg deals with a new normal, his nieces seem to help every step of the way. Take what happened after he accompanied them to the Westmoreland County Fair.

They bought a bunch of trinkets, and the next morning Greg tried to out of bed but realized he was handcuffed to it. The door in a nearby closet was slightly cracked. The giggles seeping out of the closet were all Greg needed to hear to know what his nieces had done while he was sleeping.

He was back in handcuffs. And yet he had never felt so free.

MEANING OF ISAAC

A plastic stick with a small suction cup went whizzing by my right ear. An impish and triumphant laugh followed the near miss inside of Faith Forward. The culprit had a shock of light brown hair that covered his forehead and wore a Captain Marvel T-shirt, shorts, and sandals. He looked like any four-year-old boy as he unleashed his best shot yet with a small bow. His mother, Dawn Hennessey, tried to scold him, but her own laughter undercut the attempt. Such is the miracle of Isaac, who weighed three pounds at birth but now plays and laughs like any other toddler.

Dawn and Rick Hennessey were close to adopting Isaac when I stopped at Faith Forward for a summer visit. There have been complications, but the original plan is intact: Dawn and Rick will adopt Isaac, whom they have cared for since birth, and keep his biological mother a part of his life as long as she is clean.

The progress he has made is remarkable, given that he developed later in almost every facet than most children because he was a neonatal abstinence syndrome (NAS) baby. One marker in his astounding progress came a couple of months earlier when Dawn's oldest son, Brandon, called her. His picture popped up on Dawn's cell phone, and Isaac answered it. They had a short conversation before Isaac turned the phone over to Dawn. It was a pleasant surprise since Brandon, who lives in Florida, was used to mostly baby talk from Isaac.

"When I got on the phone with Brandon, he couldn't believe Isaac was talking," Dawn said. "He didn't expect that."

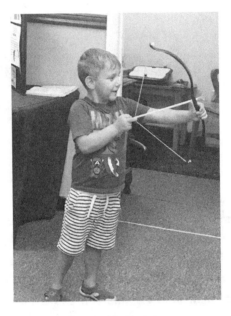

Isaac Hennessey at Faith Forward.

Dawn points to Isaac as Exhibit A in her argument that people shouldn't be hesitant to adopt NAS babies. It isn't always an easy sell. Indeed, Dawn's own mother cautioned her against it, fearing that her daughter would have to raise a handicapped child. Dawn and Rick have challenges with Isaac, but he has given them as much as they have given him.

"The purpose of this little guy goes beyond what even he realizes," Dawn said, "not just to me but it's about giving a face to children and babies born into addiction."

Isaac inspired Dawn to start Angel Arms, the network of cuddlers that helps families with NAS babies, and go beyond it.

Faith Forward is fixing up a donated Victorian-era house in Latrobe for mothers battling addiction and their children. The house needs a lot of work, but with grant money and labor supplied by volunteers, Dawn and Faith Forward are on track to providing a refuge for mothers in recovery.

Faith Forward doesn't always have to be so ambitious to make a difference. I learned that while meeting Stephanie Walker during an earlier visit to Faith Forward. Stephanie was sipping coffee and talking about her past struggles with addiction when Regina Kubreck walked into Faith Forward. Her black eye shades contrasted with her snow-white hair and gave away that she had just been to the eye doctor. Kubreck had apparently visited her hairdresser recently, too.

"Look at your 'do!" Stephanie said while rising to give her a hug and a kiss.

The two chatted while Stephanie moves closer to inspect the 'do. Regina told Stephanie she started to worry when she didn't see her earlier that week. Stephanie assured her she was fine and had simply overslept on the day she was supposed to stop by Faith Forward.

"See how they are here?" Stephanie said. "Everything here is free. The love, the counseling, the coffee."

Clean for more than three years, Stephanie attributes her recovery in part to what she found at Faith Forward. She first walked through its door in search of rent assistance after moving to the area from Delaware. The sense of family that Stephanie has received since that day is priceless.

Stephanie calls Faith Forward board member Joyce Sterling "Momma." The two are close enough for Stephanie to talk to Sterling about anything.

"If I'm wrong or acting like a spoiled brat, she'll tell me," said Stephanie, whose real mother died when she was just twenty-one. "She knows all about me."

That includes the separation from her three children because of her past drug use. It took Stephanie four trips to rehab but finally a faith-based approach worked for her. Faith Forward provides another layer of support.

"They don't make you feel like they are better than you, no matter what," Stephanie said. "That's one thing I love about Dawn. She's my family, and this is home to me. They truly care."

Stephanie talked about how she once felt such shame from her addiction that she never looked at people when she passed them on the street.

"Now, I don't walk with my head down," she said. "It's amazing. I'm just happy now."

HOPE IN ALL FORMS

During the work week, Mike Baacke gets out of bed at 4:30 every morning. As the Greensburg resident sees it, he doesn't have a choice.

"I have a lot of pressure," he said.

That pressure stems from providing for his wife and daughter, not plotting where he is going to get his next fix, something that once consumed him. Mike owns his own contracting company, buying properties and restoring and flipping houses. He aspires to have a net worth of $1 million by 2020 after starting from scratch when he dedicated himself to recovery in 2010.

Mike has made it to the other side of addiction, but he has never forgotten his old life. He is vigilant about attending Narcotics Anonymous meetings. He hires people who are in recovery and helps them manage their lives by providing loans if they are serious about long-term recovery. Mike does all of this while never losing sight of his top priority: being a good husband and father.

He never met his own father and will be damned if his kids grow up without one. He works from six to three during weekdays, so he can spend time with his baby daughter and cook his family dinner. Weekends are reserved for more family time and making improvements to his own house to build equity in it. He hopes to one day have a son and coach him in wrestling.

Against the backdrop of the opioid epidemic, he is living the American Dream.

"I wake up with a purpose," Mike said.

So does Georgette Lehr. Like Mike, Georgette is thriving in long-term recovery and helping others in addiction.

The two are proof that there are different paths to recovery as Georgette, a Uniontown resident, found hers through religion. It came after years of addiction.

Her parents divorced when Georgette was young, and she never had much of a relationship with her father. Her longing for male companionship led to promiscuity, heavy drinking, and drug experimentation. She was twenty-two when she unknowingly tried heroin for the first time. She and a boyfriend drove to Baltimore to buy cocaine. A dealer on the streets sold them heroin and said it was cocaine. Georgette didn't know any better and took it.

"I did heroin before I ever took a pain pill," she said.

By the time she started using heroin regularly, she'd lost custody of her daughter and was working at a strip club. She drank heavily so she could get through the nights she stripped. That perpetuated her addiction and low self-esteem. Georgette spent more than ten years in addiction, a decade littered with broken relationships, some of which were abusive, and abortions. She lost custody of two other daughters born during that period. Even after she acknowledged her addiction, it took ten years to turn her life around.

After embracing Jesus Christ while in a faith-based rehabilitation facility, Georgette got clean at the age of thirty-six. She rebuilt her life and relationships with the daughters she had lost. She is close with all three of them and works with others in recovery at Genesis House in Uniontown.

Georgette's biggest triumph came when she started performing with her church's worship team. She initially resisted performing on stage because it was a link to her past. A simple skit was anything but that for Georgette as it took her back to the days when she could barely look at herself in the mirror because she was so ashamed.

But she confronted the lingering demon one Sunday, and any self-loathing from being on a stage evaporated. Georgette sang and danced and realized that she could love herself as much as she loves Jesus. She finally felt free.

"I'm still on the worship team, and I sing louder than anybody," Georgette said. "What's really cool is everything is changing about how I see myself. It's weird to not think I'm disgusting, fat, and ugly, all of the things I told myself on a daily basis. That shame is finally gone. I actually think I am pretty good-looking now."

Georgette's story is different from Mike's, but their individual journeys show that there is hope amidst the opioid epidemic. Hope, as it turns out, comes in many forms.

It even comes in a bag.

* * *

Renah Kozemchak's Uncle Mike was always more like an older cousin because they were relatively close in age. They fished together, and he helped her hone her softball skills. His struggles with addiction never diminished her love for him. So she had mixed emotions as they ate lunch with other family members before he left for a drug-and-alcohol treatment center. Renah wanted nothing more than for her uncle to get well. But she would miss him and broke down in tears during their goodbyes.

"I knew I wasn't going to see him for a long time," Renah said.

A long time unfortunately turned into forever. Mike Cameron died in 2014 at the age of twenty-one of a suspected overdose. Rather than withdraw after his death, which happened while he was in treatment, Renah and her mother (Mike's sister), Dorine, decided to act.

They started Operation Passion Recovery and Hope in a Bag out of their home in Elizabeth. Hope in a Bag collects and distributes necessities, including soap, shampoo, socks, and underwear, to rehabilitation facilities in the tri-state area. Almost a year after Mike died, they delivered their first bags to rehabilitation centers and continued to grow the nonprofit organization.

"We use their bags for welcome bags," said Justin Drish, a drug-and-alcohol counselor at Teen Challenge in Cheswick. "The guys we get are coming off the street, and they have nothing."

Dorine and Renah noticed that when they visited Mike at different rehabilitation centers. Some patients didn't even own a toothbrush.

Hope in a Bag took off after Renah won third place in a national contest honoring Jackie Robinson, who is credited for breaking Major League Baseball's color barrier. Her essay on overcoming adversity and making something positive out of her uncle's death stood out among 20,000 entries.

The Pittsburgh Pirates hosted Renah and her family for a game and donated 50,000 travel shampoo bottles to their cause. The following year media personality Wendy Bell interviewed Renah for a contest among Western Pennsylvania-based charities. Her story won first place, and the $7,000 prize allowed Dorine and Renah to turn Hope in a Bag into a nonprofit organization.

Dorine and other drivers covered around 1,200 total miles, making deliveries to facilities in Pennsylvania, Ohio, and West Virginia for Christmas 2017.

"It's a lot of work," Dorine said, "but we like to do it."

TO THE MOON

Her salt-and-pepper hair was pulled into a bushy ponytail, revealing well-sculpted cheekbones and dark, expressive eyes. The nose-piercing and multiple ear-piercings made Dona Cardiff look like even less of a great-grandmother. Not that she acts like one.

She joins her grandchildren and great grandchildren when they go sledding in the fields that surround her spacious property in Mt. Pleasant. She also takes them to amusement parks—and even went on some of the rides during a trip to Kennywood Park, less than two months after getting a hip replaced. The only concession she made to the surgery that day was riding a scooter around Kennywood, so she wouldn't overdo it.

"I don't mind being seventy," Dona said. "I just don't want to be that shuffling seventy year old. If I'm shuffling, I want it to be on a dance floor."

Dona can't afford to shuffle most days since she is the primary caretaker of two great-grandchildren whose combined ages are around the square root of hers. Dona is among the grandparents who have provided stability to children who might have otherwise stayed in a dysfunctional situation or ended up in foster care.

She gained full custody of Caitlin and Delilah after she agreed to pick up their mother at a drug-and-alcohol treatment facility if she signed over custodial rights of the children to her.

Their father is Dona's grandson, and he was in prison during this time. That left Dona, who saw enough of the wild mood swings and volatility from their mother, to finally intervene. She drove straight from the rehab facility to her attorney's office, expediting the process that turned her back into a mother.

"This wasn't my plan," Dona said. "My plans for retirement were cruises and trips, to take care of me."

The abrupt change in her plans nearly overwhelmed her since Caitlin was just two and Delilah a baby when Dona assumed custody of them.

Caitlin exhibited trust and abandonment issues, residue of the turmoil she experienced as a toddler. At family gatherings, she hid behind Dona or simply stared at everyone while she played with her hands. Dona had a terrible time trying to get her to eat healthy. Caitlin only wanted crackers or potato chips, and her teeth were in such bad shape from malnutrition and neglect that she had to get one of them removed.

"When I was having trouble with Caitlin, I really thought about giving up," Dona admitted.

Change in Caitlin came gradually, and it can probably be traced to what Dona tells her great-grandchildren every chance she gets: "I love you with all my heart, to the moo-oon and back!" She said it so often that it eroded Caitlin's emotional barriers. The day Caitlin returned the saying, in a tiny voice that made moon sound more like "mewn," it nearly melted Dona.

"I left the room and cried and cried and cried," she said.

Now when Dona snuggles in bed with Delilah, Caitlin will join them. And nothing makes her change in retirement plans more worth it than those mornings when she is holding onto her great-granddaughters like she is never going to let go.

School days typically start at 7:30 with Dona calling out to Caitlin, "Time to rise and shine for school!" She makes them breakfast though Caitlin knows that if she wants pancakes to tell Dona the night before, so she can have the griddle ready.

Caitlin attends Ruffsdale Head Start, and it took many days of Dona promising she would return after dropping her at the preschool for her to settle in and enjoy school. It helps that Dona not only kept her promise but also that she volunteers at the school a couple of days a week.

Dona seems to have a limitless reservoir of energy, but she knows to pace herself. She cooks dinner the previous night or that morning and allows extra time for cleaning since the arthritis in her hands makes it harder to complete household tasks.

"What used to take me a couple of hours will take a day now," she said.

She manages though and is now getting help from her son. He moved into the garage apartment on her property after his release from prison. His work as a mechanic allows him to help financially as well. He and his girlfriend sometimes take the girls overnight to give Dona a break. The quiet time is rare and a welcome respite. But it also reinforces how much she loves having Caitlin and Delilah with her.

"They are hilarious," Dona said. "I don't get away from them a lot, but I don't mind. They are beautiful kids."

Never are they more beautiful than nights when they don't want to turn the lights out. They ask Dona—she is "Mammy" or "Ma" to them—for more hugs and kisses.

And they want to hear that she loves them with all her heart. She does and, as she tells them…To the moo-oon and back!

DRUG COURT SUCCESS

His descent into addiction followed an all-too-familiar narrative. He started smoking pot at age seventeen and began experimenting with other drugs not long after that. He moved to opiates, getting Oxycontin from an uncle or stealing from his father, who had a prescription for it. He moved to heroin after pills became too expensive. He managed—and rationalized—his habit by snorting instead of shooting heroin.

That went on for about six years before he finally took the plunge—literally.

"Once I picked a needle up, my life went to shambles," Josh Rimmel said.

Josh hit bottom when he overdosed while at home with his twelve-year-old son and eight-year-old daughter. His son called 911. The paramedics, after arriving, were just about to administer Narcan when Josh woke up. They took him to Natrona Heights Hospital, but he refused medical attention and was quickly released.

Josh had burned through so many relationships that no one would get him at the hospital. He walked for nearly two-and-a-half hours before a stranger picked him up and drove him the final five miles to his Vandergrift house. That long walk gave him time to think, time to reflect, and time to truly digest the scare he threw into his two children, right? Wrong. All Josh thought about was getting home so he could use again—to spite those who refused to get him at the hospital as much as to get a fix.

"I was that far gone in my addiction," Josh said.

Josh spent seven months in jail stemming from charges of drug paraphernalia possession and endangering children. That stint gave him the perspective he needed to want help, and he got accepted into Westmoreland County drug court.

He embraced a lengthy stay at an inpatient rehabilitation facility and further worked on his recovery at Narcotics Anonymous meetings. He made it through all five phases of drug court and graduated from the program in December 2017. The ceremony had a surreal feeling to Josh. John Blahovec, a retired judge who knew Josh all too well attended the graduation.

"It was awesome," Josh said. "He had tried and tried and tried to help me, but I just wasn't ready."

Blahovec's presence at graduation put an exclamation point on how far Josh had come from the days he spent in and out of jail for crimes that fed his addiction.

"If it wasn't tied down, I was trying to steal it for money," Josh said. "I can't tell you how many things I stole from my family for money or the cars I sold for money. I had some nice cars but sold them to the dope man for cheap just to get my next fix. That was definitely a different life, and I like to think that it wasn't me sometimes. When I was a kid, I didn't aspire to grow up to be a heroin addict."

Josh now aspires to be the best father he can be. He and his long-time girlfriend had a son, Jackson, in May 2017, about six months before Josh graduated from drug court.

"He's the highlight of my life," said Josh, who lives with his girl-friend and her two children. "He comes running to the door every day when he hears me come (home). It's great."

So is his relationship with his other two kids. They live in Kentucky with their mother but visit on holidays and during the summer. Josh said they never stopped loving him, even after seeing him overdose.

Still, it felt good when his son, now fifteen, remarked to his father about what a transformation he has made.

Josh has told his story all over the region, to students at Kiski Prep School and Penn State-New Kensington and to addicts who are living in recovery houses. He also tries to help people who have relapsed after graduating from drug court. Josh reserved a bed for one of them at Spirit Life outside of Indiana and told the man he would pay to keep it reserved for whenever he is ready for help.

Josh remains committed to his own sobriety and attends at least four Narcotics Anonymous meetings a week.

"That's what got me to where I'm at," he said of the time he puts into recovery. "I can't drop it just because I'm not doing some program. Drug court helped, but that's not what's going to keep me clean. I've got to keep doing the things I did to get to where I'm at."

Drug court hasn't only had a profound effect on successful graduates, such as Josh.

It has also changed Judge Meagan Bilick-DeFazio's outlook. While working as a public defender early in her career, Bilik-DeFazio concluded that heroin addiction was either a death sentence or a continual string of jail sentences.

"I never really saw anybody get clean," said Bilik-DeFazio, who now oversees Westmoreland County drug court with Judge Christopher Feliciani. "To see the good come out of (drug court) is really enlightening, and it makes you want to work harder. I've learned so much in doing this."

She paused and laughed. "I'm the most paranoid parent on earth now," she said.

Bilik-DeFazio doesn't just joke about how drug court changed her perspective as a mother. Bilik-DeFazio started drug testing her daughter when she turned twelve. "And for my son, it may be even sooner," she said.

Drug testing at an early age gets her kids used to it and gives them an out if they face peer pressure to try drugs. They can blame it on their "crazy" mother if someone offers them something they decline to take. If they do fall into drug use, it will be caught at an early age and confronted.

As Bilik-DeFazio sees it, her approach merely reflects health precautions she takes with her children.

"We use sunscreen, and we drug test," she said.

Bilik-DeFazio advocates mandatory testing for students who participate in extracurricular activities. She believes such measures are necessary because of how times have changed since she graduated from high school in 1993. Back then, drugs weren't as prevalent as they are now, Bilik-DeFazio said. One of the things that has surprised her the most about drug court is hearing how participants started drinking and using marijuana as kids and quickly moved to harder drugs. To Bilick-DeFazio, this confirms how much the landscape has changed.

"There's all kinds of stuff accessible to (kids) that's even easier to get than beer," she said. "If your kids are in the frame of mind where they're willing to smoke something or snort something, it's only a matter of time. You really have to be a different parent than our parents were because there was pot around and alcohol around back then, but that was about it."

CASEY'S LEGACY

She heard the sirens and figured it was just New York City. Michelle Schwartzmier started to worry when she saw helicopters hovering in the sky. Then one of the women she was with received a text message from a friend telling her to get out of there. They were a block from where a bomb exploded in the subway.

Michelle has continued telling the story of her daughter, Casey, and not even a suspected terrorist attack will stop her. She taped a public service announcement that day for Partnership for Drug-Free Kids that took *eight* hours. Her so-called vacation also included participation in a fundraiser that raised a million dollars for a hotline for addicts and their families. More significant (if less dramatic) is what Michelle has done closer to her home in the North Hills of Pittsburgh. When I got caught up with her three months after we met she had recently achieved a breakthrough in her fight to shatter the stigma of addiction.

She spoke at North Hills High School, Casey's alma mater, with her husband and son among those in the audience. Michelle said it was the first time North Hills had ever done anything like that. She also participated in a program at North Allegheny, a neighboring school district, for eighth-grade girls to prepare them for high school. She left that day exhausted and a little overwhelmed. A week later, the school's superintendent called Michelle to tell her about student comments from surveys that were taken.

Some wrote how powerful Michelle was and that she changed the way they looked at things. Others thanked her for being honest and talking about something their parents were afraid to discuss. Michelle was relieved because she worried that she'd been a little too honest, based on the number of girls she saw crying. The call from the superintendent validated the blunt approach she takes in telling her story.

"We need to do this," Michelle said. "We need to slap them in the face with reality."

Michelle gets that every day while grieving the loss of a child. Christmas, a couple of months earlier, was her first one without Casey. Not only that, it brought back painful memories of the previous Christmas. There had been a real feeling of hope that Casey, who was set to go to a rehabilitation center in California, was ready to conquer her demons once and for all.

"I was dreading the build up to Christmas," Michelle said. "The weeks leading up to it, I was thinking, 'My God, how do I do this? How do I have Christmas without her?' I wanted to sit in bed and cry, but I can't. I have a son who needs Christmas, and he's lost enough. I can't take that from him."

In May, Michelle and her husband, Richard, went to the cemetery on what would have been Casey's 21st birthday and released balloons in her memory. They celebrated a couple of weeks later when Eric picked Robert Morris for college. He is studying actuary sciences and living on campus. He could have lived at home, but Michelle encouraged him to embrace the whole college experience. Plus, she knows she will see enough of him with Robert Morris only forty minutes away.

The grave where she and her husband released balloons produced the kind of story that keeps Michelle going.

She received a message from a man who had been jogging through the cemetery when he saw that a snowstorm had toppled an angel statue from one of the graves. He stopped to fix it and noticed Casey's grave. He was drawn to her picture and how young she was when she died. He memorized her name and later went online and found her story. He sent a message to Michelle about how the chance encounter empowered him. He said that he was an addict and that when he jogs past Casey's grave, he will stop and say a prayer.

"What you have done for me and what Casey has done is a miracle," he wrote of the hope he received from the experience. The message left Michelle in tears, and what she hears from people in addiction inspires her.

Michelle and Casey Schwartzmier. Photo courtesy of Michelle Schwartzmier.

During a recent talk at a rehabilitation facility, the group invited her to stay for lunch. She ate and joked with them and felt as comfortable as if they were her own family members. A few of them asked if they could chat with her in private. They just needed someone to talk to, someone to listen to them. Someone who understood them.

"When I'm sitting there with these addicts, I feel connected to them on such a deep level," Michelle said. It is one of the ways she stays close to Casey.

The most poignant connection can be seen in a scrapbook that Miranda Caryll, one of Casey's friends, made shortly after her death. It started with a Facebook group post about Casey's obituary in which

Miranda asked people to send pictures that she could put in a scrapbook. She received pictures from all over the world. One was taken in front of Buckingham Palace in London; another was taken on the Yellow Brick Road in Kansas. One man took his picture in front of a rehabilitation center with the message that Casey had inspired him to seek help.

All of the pictures showed people holding a card that said, in some form, that Casey's story had reached them. All fifty states in the United States were represented. Some of the pictures came from as far away as Japan and Pakistan.

The project was particularly meaningful to Miranda because she and Casey had talked about seeing the world together with another friend, who died from an overdose a year and a half before Casey. When Miranda presented the scrapbook to Michelle, she told her, "I want you to see that Casey did travel the world after all." There is a picture of a key on the scrapbook cover accompanied by a passage: *Your story can be the key that unlocks someone else's nightmare.*

Looking at the scrapbook gives Michelle a feeling of *saudade.*

"It is one of many things that makes me smile through the tears," Michelle said. "It's amazing that this twenty-year-old girl from Pittsburgh, who many times during her struggle felt that nobody cared about her, has done wonderful things."

A different scrapbook reinforces to Michelle the need to continue her work as an activist. For Casey's eighteen birthday, Michelle made a scrapbook with the quote, "The best is yet to come." Every page commemorated a year in her life, and Casey took the scrapbook with her every time she went to a rehabilitation center. It was a reminder of what she was fighting for as she tried to overcome her addiction.

Michelle was reminded of both scrapbooks one day when she came across a Facebook post that Casey wrote a few years earlier. Casey talked about how badly she wanted to do great things with her life but wondered if she would ever get that chance.

"She was broken and trying to get out of this evilness," Michelle said. "I read that now and think, 'Oh God, baby girl, you did something good. It's okay.'"

Indeed, Casey's story continues to resonate with people all over the world.

When Michelle posted a thank you to all who contributed pictures to the scrapbook, her Facebook account was flooded with messages, some in languages she didn't recognize. After Michelle wrote a blog post for Partnership for Drug-Free Kids, someone from the organization's IT department told her it received the most hits in the history of the website.

A couple of weeks after talking with Michelle, she sent me a text message. She'd been online and came across one of her quotes that Partnership for Drug-Free Kids posted on its site: "Whether you have someone you love who is struggling or have already lost them, you're not alone. You have others around who have walked the same path. Reach out to them."

It was continued affirmation to keep the promise Michelle made to Casey to tell her story, in the hope of reaching others.

"I see articles about Casey or me that I didn't know existed, and it stops me in my tracks every time," she wrote in the text.

She concluded the short message with this: "Wow . . . go Casey! Keep it moving baby girl."

EPILOGUE

The first half of 2018 produced encouraging news in Westmoreland County. There were only sixty-one overdose deaths through six months, according to the county coroner's office, after a record 193 in 2017. Unfortunately, there were ten overdose deaths in the first week of July, including four on the Fourth of July. That spate of fatalities underscored why Tim Phillips, executive director of the Westmoreland County Drug Overdose Task Force, is cautiously optimistic, if not dismissive, of statistics that show progress in the opioid epidemic battle. "We're so focused on the damn numbers that sometimes we forget the families and communities affected by loss," Tim said.

Both suffered a tragic loss on July 4 when Gary Josebeck died of a heroin overdose. A talented artist and musician, Gary started Art and Recovery for Transformation, a group that promotes art for people to express themselves without using drugs. His death hit the recovery community hard.

Tim was close with Gary. Like others, he was left with more questions than answers after Gary's death, one month after his twenty-sixth birthday. Tim wondered if Gary isolated himself after relapsing, given his stature in the recovery community.

"There's no shame in relapsing," Tim said. "We understand that it happens. The real shame is not doing anything about it."

I reconnected with Tim and Tony Marcocci, a longtime county detective who is also on the task force, six months after meeting them for the first time. I was curious to see what, if anything, had changed. Both said progress is being made, though too slow for their liking. Each reiterated that the battle is a slog since there are no easy answers to a complex problem.

As an example of just how rooted the problem is, Tim said he is getting requests from Head Start preschools to talk to kids. Some kids are seeing parents do drugs, which makes educating them early about the dangers of drugs imperative.

"It's a tough one," Tim said of talking to children so young about drugs. "But we need to give them the information to make safe and healthy choices."

The need to talk to children earlier and earlier is because drug use shows no signs of abating.

"The general public doesn't know what's going on in the streets of Greensburg," Tony said. "They don't have a clue."

Tony and Tim echoed many of the same sentiments they expressed when we first met:

- Westmoreland County has a glaring need for inpatient treatment facilities and sober-living homes (there was just one of each when this book went to press).

- Stigma remains one of the biggest obstacles to making progress because it deters addicts and families from getting help.

- Addicts must be given a chance to succeed in long-term recovery through job opportunities and some form of driving privileges if they don't have them.

Tim is hopeful that Pathways to Pardons, an initiative headed by former Pennsylvania Lt. Governor Mike Stack, will help addicts who are in recovery but hindered by their past. He worked with Stack's staff on the program that will expunge records for some crimes if certain requirements are met.

"It's a step in the right direction," Tim said.

Tim places onus on recovering addicts, too, as far as helping themselves. He said they have to accept that managing their sobriety is something they will always do, no matter how far in the rearview mirror they put their addiction. Tim exemplifies this. In recovery for almost thirty years, he still attends 12-step meetings regularly and does not take his sobriety for granted.

"Complacency is the enemy to staying clean, and I see that a lot," Tim said. "People reach these milestones and start thinking, *I beat it.* No, we have a chronic disease. We've just got today, and we've got to do whatever we can today to stay clean. We can't stay clean today on what we did yesterday."

* * *

Project Stand prompted Dawn Hennessey to pray. It also caused her to shed a few tears. And that was *before* the annual event that Faith Forward stages to rally the community against the opioid epidemic.

Rain tormented Western Pennsylvania all summer, and the weather, the one thing Dawn couldn't control, wasn't expected to cooperate with Project Stand. But the mid-August day brought mostly blue skies though humidity that stuck like Scotch tape. Dawn was all smiles when I caught up with her later in the day at Legion Keener Park in Latrobe, and not just because the weather held up.

"Do you feel the energy?" she asked.

It was indeed palpable at an event that felt part revival and part carnival, complete with a bouncy house and games for kids. There were tables and tents offering information and help. There was a stage set among a clearing of trees that hosted a parade of speakers and musical performers throughout the day. Judges, politicians, religious leaders, and people in long-term recovery were among those who addressed the crowd with stories of heartbreak and hope.

James Bumar at Project Stand shortly before he
retired as police chief of Latrobe.

A large prayer circle formed early in the afternoon. The prayer was followed by a balloon release to remember those who lost their battle with addiction and support those still struggling with it.

One speaker, William Urbanik, may have best summed up the gathering that drew more than 1,000 people.

"Here's an issue we can all rally behind," Urbanik told me shortly before he took the stage.

To Urbanik, a financial advisor and publisher of a local magazine, the opioid epidemic transcends politics. It is one issue that shouldn't divide or polarize people because it is as simple as life or death. Urbanik and his wife started *GOAL Magazine* in 2016 to cover Westmoreland County trends and happenings and support charitable endeavors.

The following year, *GOAL* hosted the "We Are at War" symposium at St. Vincent College. The event stemmed partly from what Urbanik saw happening. People were dying, and they weren't the stereotypical addicts living under a bridge. As a father of twin sons, it terrified him.

But he refused to look the other way or adopt the won't-happen-to-me mindset that many believe still permeates the country.

"So, I started talking about it," Urbanik said of the opioid epidemic.

Talking about it is one of the most important things to breaking the stigma that keeps addicts and their families in the shadows, too ashamed to seek help. As Tim Phillips told the crowd, "Stigma kills people. This is a treatable, curable disease."

Shannon Moore, another of the Project Stand speakers, is proof of that. Clean for thirty-three months, Shannon's own mother didn't think she'd live past twenty. She has "July 16" tattooed down her right forearm to signify when she resolved to change.

That November Shannon finally got clean because she feared she had cheated death one too many times. She later spent almost eleven months in prison from an earlier dealing arrest but stuck with her sobriety. To help ensure she stays sober, Shannon requested a five-year probation upon her release from prison. She has since been subject to frequent drug tests and other safeguards. At age thirty-eight, she now searches her teenage son and his friends before they enter her apartment to check for drugs.

While clean herself, the opioid epidemic's undertow continues to plague Shannon. She lost a handful of friends to overdoses in the summer of 2018. One of those came on July 4 when her friend, Beth Pugner, died from an overdose at fifty-one. Beth left behind three kids, including a daughter who grew up with Shannon's son. It was another blow to Shannon, who has lost more than two hundred friends or acquaintances, many to drug- or alcohol-related deaths.

That reality is why Shannon often looks at her tattoo. It symbolizes recovery in many ways. It reminds Shannon that's when she wanted to change, after two decades in addiction, not when she got clean for good. Her recovery wasn't linear. Nor was it easy. But Shannon wants to be an example to her son and keep him from going down the path that probably should have killed her. She wants to live, a feeling that is reinforced with so many around her dying.

"I don't want to go back to where I was," said Shannon, who plans to return to school. "My tattoo reminds me to never give up."

The same could be said for Dawn after Project Stand.

From her perspective, the day couldn't have gone much better. It was a community coming together to celebrate life, not dwell on the destruction caused by the opioid epidemic. The hope that Dawn preached, whether she was on stage or talking to people as she made rounds at Project Stand, could be found at the bouncy house.

Isaac, the neo-natal abstinence baby who barely survived his birth, spent most of the day at the house and the games set up near it. Isaac laughed and played and always seemed to find his way back to the bouncy house line, so he could take another turn.

He was just like any four-year-old boy.

A couple of weeks later, Dawn and Rick moved closer to officially making Isaac their son. An adoption hearing that had them so anxious they spent the day before it crying in their attorney's office, went in their favor. Barring any unforeseen developments, the adoption would become official at a final hearing in December.

Isaac has been with the Hennesseys since birth and is too young to grasp all that went into his adoption. He did understand what it meant when Dawn and Rick told him they would have a party to "celebrate Isaac." The guest of honor got to pick the menu, and Isaac wanted donuts, potato chips, and French fries, not necessarily in that order.

Dawn was reminded of the larger purpose of Isaac *while* she testified in the adoption hearing. Judge John Driscoll stopped testimony at one point and started asking her questions about Angel Arms. That lasted for about twenty minutes and ended with Dawn providing Driscoll with contact information for the nonprofit organization.

Inquiries about Angel Arms have extended far beyond a Westmoreland County courtroom. Since the *700 Club* aired a piece on Angel Arms in May 2018, the organization has received calls from all over the country. Dawn had recently gotten a call from someone in Costa Rica and was working with a group in the eastern part of the state that wants to start an organization based on Angel Arms.

Angel Arms was also in the process of starting a twenty-four-hour hotline that will provide help for NAS babies who need to be rescued or simply give advice for distressed parents who can't get their baby to stop crying. To Dawn, Angel Arms' growth all goes back to Isaac and what she has learned from him. That made particularly fitting what she told Isaac one day when he asked if he had been in her "tummy." Dawn and Rick have vowed to be truthful with Isaac about his past. That day Dawn explained that Isaac had been in his biological mother's tummy.

That God had given him to her as a special gift.

* * *

Losing someone he helped is always gut-wrenching. But Gary Josebeck's death hit Carmen Capozzi particularly hard. He has known Gary's mother for years, and she called Carmen when his drug problem first surfaced. Carmen, who started Sage's Army in 2012 after losing his son to an overdose, talked Gary into going to an inpatient rehabilitation facility. The two became close, and Gary frequently wore a black Sage's Army T-shirt. The shirt was draped over the casket at Gary's viewings, and when Carmen saw it he broke down crying. Gary's death also stirred something in Carmen that put him back at odds with himself.

He'd scaled back at Sage's Army to take time for himself to address some issues, including post-traumatic stress disorder (PTSD). Carmen never really grieved Sage's death, instead charging into grassroots activism. He and his longtime partner, Cindy, built Sage's Army into one of the most impactful organizations of its kind in Western Pennsylvania. But the exhausting pace at which Carmen battled the epidemic, both emotionally and physically, caught up with him in early 2018 at a parent/coach training session in Harrisburg.

During a meditation exercise, Carmen was hit with a wave of grief and lost control of his emotions. Like a dam bursting, the pain from Sage's death poured out as Carmen cried uncontrollably. Shortly after that, he started seeing a counselor and stepped back from Sage's Army to concentrate on himself. Mornings readings, often from the Bible, became a staple of his days. He and Cindy took a couple of short vacations. Carmen is still in counseling and working through grief that will never dissipate.

"I'm just as fragile as some of the people that I'm helping," Carmen said. "Probably the biggest thing I have learned through all of this is how important self-care is."

Gary's death may test that. Carmen was angry with himself after Gary died, wondering if he could have done more to help him had he not stepped back from Sage's Army. That thinking reenergized him and compelled him to return to activism. It also raised a question: Can he strike a balance between his work through Sage's Army and everything else?

"I can't save the world," said Carmen, who also owns a flooring business. "I am learning to step back."

He is doing so with an eye toward an ambitious project. Carmen plans to open houses for people in recovery, and funding is in place to start the first one. But, in trying to balance his health and his involvement, he wants a team in place before he starts the project.

When we talked, the Centers for Disease Control and Prevention (CDC) had just announced that more than 72,000 people in the United States died from a drug overdose in 2017, up more than six percent from the previous year. Carmen is concerned that such statistics are losing their shock value, that people are getting used to overdose deaths as a way of life.

"My biggest fear is people are just tuning it out," Carmen said.

People like Carmen don't have that option. He deals with constant reminders of what he lost when Sage died, and he never knows when he will encounter them. Watching TV recently, he quickly changed the channel because the program featured grandparents. Carmen couldn't bear to watch it for one simple reason.

"I will never have grandchildren," he said.

* * *

Diana Shea laughed as she talked about her nine-year-old daughter on a lazy August afternoon. Shyanna was out catching insects with other kids from her Kittanning neighborhood, enjoying the dwindling summer vacation days. Diana reveled in the innocence of it, even if she didn't know what creatures Shyanna might bring home.

Diana celebrated her third year clean in July 2018. She has stayed on top of her sobriety by regularly attending 12-step meetings. When she had five teeth pulled, she refused a painkiller prescription. She told the dentist that she is in recovery, and he told her how proud he was of her. It was another marker in how far she has come.

"It does get easier," Diana said of recovery. "Things get better as you go along."

Diana still carries daily reminders of where addiction took her so she doesn't return to using. There is the jail identification bracelet. There are the before and after driver's license pictures. She looks so different in them that once she almost ran into a problem while trying to claim a certified letter at the post office. It happened before she renewed her license, and the ID she gave looked nothing like her. Her skin was pale, her eyes lifeless. Not anymore. Diana kept her old license to show people the life of addiction.

Before recovery and after driver's license pictures of Diana Shea.
Photos courtesy of Diana Shea.

Diana continues to tell her story and is considering becoming a certified recovery specialist or a certified peer specialist. In the meantime, she uses poetry as an outlet and has filled notebooks that detail her struggle with addiction and the joy of sobriety. I asked her to send me a poem, and she didn't hesitate with what she wanted to share.

Addiction is like a tsunami,
hits hard and long,
does so much damage, and takes too many lives.
For many, it's so hard to bear the surprise;
takes so many to rebuild the place it washed away.
It's hard to take it day by day,
to keep it simple and real.
People saved can have a chance at a new deal;
having faith is all you really need
Time will improve, most indeed
care for those who lost, and those in need.
God bless all and all God speed.

AFTERWORD

The irony of writing a book about the opioid epidemic is that I learned more about it than I ever could have by reading a book. I hope what distinguishes this project is the people and their stories that bring it all together. Their experiences cover all aspects of the epidemic. They humanize this book.

I stayed away from editorializing because I want readers to draw their own conclusions from those impacted by the epidemic. I would love for this to be the equivalent of a presentation that stays with readers long after the final page is turned.

Parents need to know what they are facing, and that includes prescribed opiates, and what to do if their child falls prey to addiction. Children need to know how drastic a turn their lives take if they start using and abusing opiates. Even if they make it to the other side of addiction, without doing extensive damage to their future and family relationships, recovery is something they will have to manage for their rest of their lives. Is that worth plunging a needle into your arm? That is may be a stark way to put it, but that is how quickly things can escalate.

That so many people fall into use is proof that such decisions don't happen in a vacuum. Some people do it because they aren't mature enough or are too are impaired to see the long-term ramifications or both. Others make the decision because they are masking the kind of pain that doesn't always show up in an MRI. There are many reasons why people abuse drugs. One I've never heard is that someone simply aspired to be an addict.

I would hope that people who read this book won't be so quick to judge because it can happen to anybody. That is why I am so appreciative to Kevin Stevens for writing the introduction to the book.

Kevin leverages the name he made during a successful NHL career to spread his story of addiction and recovery. His voice is an important one because of two overarching messages: if it can happen to him, it can happen to anybody—and don't be so quick to judge. Stigma is addiction's oxygen as it keeps too many people suffering from it in the shadows, whether it is addicts who are too ashamed to seek help or family members who won't talk about a loved one battling addiction out of fear that they'll be judged.

We are in the midst of a national crisis, the kind that demands a call to action. And yet the biggest contribution many can make doesn't require a time or financial commitment. It is simply changing, or at least challenging, their mindset when it comes to addicts.

Remember these are human beings, not statistics. They love, hurt, dream, bleed, and make mistakes.

Just like all of us.

* * *

To those looking for help, I have included a list of organizations that were a part of the book. This is by no means a complete list of all the resources out there. Even if an organization listed below may not be the right fit for someone, it will direct that person to the place where he or she can get help.

Partnership for Drug-Free Kids

1–855–378–4373

www.drugfree.org

Substance Abuse and Mental Health Services Administration

1–800–662–4357 (national helpline)

www.samhsa.org

Westmoreland County Drug Overdose Task Force

2 N. Main Street, Suite 101

Greensburg, PA 15601

724–830–3827

Westmoreland Drug and Alcohol Commission

1200 Maronda Way, Suite 300

Monessen, PA 15062

724–243–2220

1–800–220–1810 (24-hour hotline)

Southwestern Pennsylvania Heath Services

203 South Maple Avenue

Greensburg, PA 15601

1–800–220–1810 (24-hour hotline)

Sage's Army

216 4th Street

Irwin, PA 15642

724–863–5433 (24-hour hotline)

www.sagesarmy.com

Faith Forward/Angel Arms

338 Main Street

Latrobe, PA 15650

724–539–7900

faithforwardpa@gmail.com

Lost Dreams Awakening
408 8th St., Rear Suites
New Kensington, PA 15068
724–594–7670

Medmark Treatment Center
1037 Compass Circle
Greensburg, PA 15601
724–834–1144

Residents Against Illicit Drugs
P.O. Box 306
North Apollo, PA 15673
724–787–4514

Allegheny Recovery Krew
3228 Provost Road
Pittsburgh, PA 15227
412–403–9084

Save the Michaels of the World
P.O. Box 55
Buffalo, NY 14207
716–984–8375
www.savethemichaels.org

atTAcK Addiction
P.O. Box 36
Bear, DE 19701
302–593–0949
www.attackaddiction.org

Bridge to the Mountains
2700 Jane Street
Pittsburgh, PA 15203–2315
www.bridgetothemountains.org

ABOUT THE AUTHOR

Scott Brown is an author and free-lance writer who has written eight books, including *Miracle in the Making: The Adam Taliaferro Story, Heaven Sent: The Heather Miller Story* and *Pittsburgh Steelers Fans' Bucket List.* His book *In The Locker Room with Tunch Ilkin* was published in October 2018. Brown previously covered the Steelers for the *Pittsburgh Tribune-Review* and ESPN and also worked for *Florida Today* and *The Philadelphia Inquirer.* He lives in Greensburg, Pennsylvania.

For more information: go to the Hope & Heartbreak: Beyond The Numbers Of The Opioid Epidemic Facebook page.

NOTES

NOTES

NOTES

NOTES

NOTES